OCCASIONAL PAPER 269

Fiscal Implications of the Global Economic and Financial Crisis

By a Staff Team from the Fiscal Affairs Department

INTERNATIONAL MONETARY FUND

Washington DC

2009

Production: IMF Multimedia Services Division
Figures: Theodore F. Peters, Jr.
Typesetting: Alicia Etchebarne-Bourdin

Cataloging-in-Publication Data

Fiscal implications of the global economic and financial crisis/by a staff team from the Fiscal Affairs Dept.—Washington, D.C.: International Monetary Fund, 2009.

    p.   cm.—Occasional paper (International Monetary Fund); no. 269.

Includes bibliographical references.
ISBN 978-1-58906-850-6

1. Global Financial Crisis, 2008–2009. 2. Fiscal policy. 3. Economic stabilization. 4. Finance, Public. 5. Debts, Public. I. International Monetary Fund. Fiscal Affairs Dept. II. Title. III. Series: Occasional Paper (International Monetary Fund); no. 269.

HB3722.F573   2009

Please send orders to:
International Monetary Fund, Publication Services
700 19th Street, N.W., Washington, D.C. 20431, U.S.A.
Tel.: (202) 623-7430   Fax: (202) 623-7201
E-mail: publications@imf.org
Internet: www.imfbookstore.org

Contents

The following conventions are used in this publication:

- In tables, a blank cell indicates "not applicable," ellipsis points (. . .) indicate "not available," and 0 or 0.0 indicates "zero" or "negligible." Minor discrepancies between sums of constituent figures and totals are due to rounding.

- An en dash (–) between years or months (for example, 2007–08 or January–June) indicates the years or months covered, including the beginning and ending years or months; a slash or virgule (/) between years or months (for example, 2007/08) indicates a fiscal or financial year, as does the abbreviation FY (for example, FY2008).

- "Billion" means a thousand million; "trillion" means a thousand billion.

- "Basis points" refer to hundredths of 1 percentage point (for example, 25 basis points are equivalent to ¼ of 1 percentage point).

As used in this publication, the term "country" does not in all cases refer to a territorial entity that is a state as understood by international law and practice. As used here, the term also covers some territorial entities that are not states but for which statistical data are maintained on a separate and independent basis.

Preface

The global financial crisis is having major implications for the public finances of most countries. Direct fiscal support is being provided to the financial sector. Fiscal revenues are declining through the operation of automatic stabilizers and because of lower asset and commodity prices. Many countries are undertaking discretionary fiscal stimulus. The consequent fiscal deterioration is particularly strong for advanced countries, where the increase in both government debt and contingent liabilities is unprecedented in scale and pervasiveness since the end of the Second World War. Moreover, these developments are taking place in the context of severe long-run fiscal challenges, especially for countries facing rapid population aging.

The fiscal balances of G-20 advanced countries are projected to weaken by 8 percentage points of GDP on average, and government debt is projected to rise by 20 percentage points of GDP in 2008–09, with most of the deterioration occurring in 2009. The fiscal balances of G-20 emerging market economies will deteriorate by 5 percentage points of GDP. For advanced economies, the increase in debt mostly reflects support to the financial sector, fiscal stimulus, and revenue losses caused by the crisis. For emerging economies, a relatively large component of the fiscal weakening reflects declining commodity and asset prices. Collapsing asset prices have also had adverse effects on funded components of pension systems, with potentially significant risks for public accounts over the next few years.

While fiscal balances are expected to improve over the medium term, they will remain weaker than before the crisis. Public debt-to-GDP ratios will continue to increase over the medium term: in 2014 the G-20 advanced country average is projected to exceed the end-2007 average by 36 percentage points of GDP. On current policies, debt ratios will continue to grow over the longer term, reflecting demographic forces. Moreover, for both advanced and emerging economies, the crisis has increased short- and medium-term fiscal risks, with key downside risks arising from the need for possible further support to the financial sector, the intensity and the persistence of the output downturn, and the return from the management and sale of assets acquired during the financial support operations.

This somber fiscal outlook raises issues of fiscal solvency, and could eventually trigger adverse market reactions. This must be avoided: market confidence in governments' solvency is a key source of stability and a precondition for economic recovery. Therefore, there is an urgent need for governments to clarify their strategy to ensure that solvency is not at risk. In formulating such a strategy, four components are particularly important: (1) fiscal stimulus packages, where these are appropriate, should not have permanent effects on deficits; (2) medium-term frameworks, buttressed by clearly identified policies and supportive institutional arrangements, should provide a commitment to fiscal correction, once economic conditions improve; (3) structural reforms should be implemented to enhance growth; and (4) countries facing demographic pressures should firmly commit to clear strategies for health and pension reforms. While these prescriptions are not new, the weaker state of public finances has dramatically raised the cost of inaction.

This Occasional Paper was prepared by a staff team from the Fiscal Affairs Department headed by Carlo Cottarelli and comprising S. M. Ali Abbas, Steven Barnett, Thomas Baunsgaard, Jacques Bouhga-Hagbe, Giovanni Callegari, Stephanie Eble, Julio Escolano, Annalisa Fedelino, Manal Fouad, Robert Gillingham, Mark Horton, Anna Ivanova, Jiri Jonas, Philippe D. Karam, Daehaeng Kim, Manmohan Kumar, Daniel Leigh, Adam

Leive, Lusine Lusinyan, Edouard Martin, Paolo Mauro, Steven Symansky, Elsa Sze, Anita Tuladhar, and Daria Zakharova, assisted by Sukhmani Bedi, Maria Coelho, Maria David, and Annette Kyobe. Esha Ray of the External Relations Department coordinated production of the publication.

An earlier version of the paper ("The State of Public Finances: Outlook and Medium-Term Policies After the 2008 Crisis") was discussed by the IMF's Executive Board at a seminar on February 20, 2009. The opinions expressed in the paper are those of the authors, however, and do not necessarily reflect the views of the national authorities, the IMF, or IMF Executive Directors.

Abbreviations

AMLF	Asset-Backed Commercial Paper Money Market Mutual Fund Liquidity Facility
APS	Asset Protection Scheme
CAP	Capital Assistance Program
CBO	Congressional Budget Office
CCA	Contingent claims approach
CDC	Caisse des Dépôts et Consignations
CDS	Credit default swap
CIT	Corporate income tax
CP	Commercial paper
CPFF	Commercial Paper Funding Facility
CPP	Capital Purchase Program
CPS	Cost-pressure scenario
EC	European Commission
ECB	European Central Bank
EDC	Export Development Corporation
EDF	Expected default frequency
EICDS	Expected default frequency implied credit default swap
ESA	European System of Accounts
ESF	Exchange Stabilization Fund
EU	European Union
FDIC	Federal Deposit Insurance Corporation
FHA	Federal Housing Administration
FSP	Financial Stability Plan
G-20	Group of 20 countries
GAO	Government Accountability Office
GDP	Gross domestic product
GFSM	*Government Finance Statistics Manual*
GSE	Government-sponsored enterprise
JDIC	Japan Deposit Insurance Corporation
LGD	Loss given default
LIBOR	London interbank offered rate
MBS	Mortgage-backed securities
MMIF	Money Market Investor Funding Facility
MYEFO	Mid-Year Economic and Fiscal Outlook
OECD	Organization for Economic Cooperation and Development
OMB	Office of Management and Budget
PBGC	Pension Benefit Guaranty Corporation
PDCF	Primary Dealer Credit Facility
PPIF	Public-Private Investment Fund
PIT	Personal income tax
PPF	Pension Protection Fund
PPP	Purchasing power parity
PPIP	Public-Private Investment Program
PRA	Purchase and resale agreement

RBS	Royal Bank of Scotland
RMBS	Residential mortgage-backed securities
SME	Small and medium-sized enterprise
SNDO	Swedish National Debt Office
TAF	Term Auction Facility
TALF	Term Asset-Backed Securities Loan Facility
TARP	Troubled Asset Relief Program
TLGP	Temporary Liquidity Guarantee Program
VAT	Value-added tax
WEO	*World Economic Outlook*

I Overview

The financial and economic crisis is affecting the fiscal accounts of virtually all IMF members through several channels. First, many countries have supported the financial sector directly, primarily through "below-the-line" operations affecting governments' assets and liabilities, as well as operations giving rise to contingent liabilities. Second, the growth deceleration, coupled with asset and commodity price declines, is affecting revenues (and, in some cases, spending). Third, discretionary stimulus has been used to support aggregate demand. Moreover, the losses suffered by funded pension schemes may involve contingent liabilities for the state. For many countries, these developments come in the context of a projected long-term deterioration in fiscal balances reflecting demographic changes. Indeed, in these countries, fiscal policy before the crisis was expected to focus on prepositioning the fiscal accounts to make room for increased aging-related spending. The opposite has happened.

It is now critical to reassess the state of public finances in light of the crisis and pursue strategies to ensure fiscal solvency. Major doubts about fiscal solvency would lead to a surge in risk premia on government paper, destabilize expectations, and further shake market confidence. A clear strategy to ensure fiscal solvency is, therefore, an important element for the resolution of the current crisis.

This paper quantifies the fiscal implications of the crisis, assesses the status of fiscal balances after the shock, and discusses the strategy to ensure fiscal solvency. The focus is primarily on advanced and emerging market economies, complementing the recent paper on the effect of the crisis on low-income countries.[1] While, for practical purposes, some of the empirical evidence presented refers only to the G-20 countries, information is provided also for other countries, and the analysis also applies to them.[2] Section II estimates the fiscal costs and contingent liabilities arising from direct support extended to financial institutions and markets, looking both at the upfront gross costs and the likely recovery from asset sales. Section III assesses the budget impact of the recession related to the automatic stabilizers, other nondiscretionary effects (e.g., revenue losses from asset price declines), and the discretionary stimulus. Section IV looks at fiscal risks arising from the losses suffered by funded pension schemes. Section V presents the overall fiscal outlook for advanced and emerging economies, adding together the effects discussed in the earlier sections, and discusses risks to the baseline. The projections are based on the IMF's April 2009 *World Economic Outlook*. Section VI assesses the outlook for fiscal solvency, calls for the early identification of a fiscal strategy to ensure solvency, and outlines the key components of such a strategy. The Appendixes include supporting material. As a general caveat, the estimates presented are subject to a significant degree of uncertainty, and developments should be closely monitored as new information becomes available.

---

[1]See IMF (2009).

[2]The G-20 group is defined in this paper as inclusive of Spain.

II   Fiscal Implications of the Crisis: Direct Costs

Government support to the financial sector can take various forms, with different implications for gross and net debt. Operations undertaken directly by the government typically entail an upfront rise in gross government debt, though not necessarily a change in net worth and the deficit, given the related acquisition of assets. Over time, the fiscal impact will critically depend on the realization value of the acquired assets (i.e., recoveries from their sale). Other operations—those undertaken by the central bank or guarantees—have less immediate implications for the fiscal accounts, but may also have important costs over the medium term. For all, a transparent treatment in the fiscal accounts is necessary (see Box 2.1 and Appendix I).

Headline Support to Financial Sectors[3]

Advanced Countries

Many advanced countries have provided, or announced the intent to provide, significant support to their financial sectors. Support measures have varied markedly in extent and nature (see Table 2.1 and Appendix II). Estimates in Table 2.1 are based on official announcements of amounts allocated for financial sector support (or the maximum amount of banks' liabilities to be guaranteed), although they may not be used in full.[4] However, data on central bank operations reflect actual changes in the balance sheets since June 2007.

- *Capital injections.* Many countries have recapitalized their banks, particularly the systemically important ones. For the advanced G-20 countries, the average outlay to date is projected at $3\frac{1}{2}$ percent of GDP, with considerable variation across countries (ranging from 5.2 percent in the United States to none for Australia, Canada, and Spain). Among smaller advanced economies, Austria, Belgium, Ire-

land, and the Netherlands have announced large programs, ranging from $3\frac{1}{2}$ to 6 percent of GDP.

- *Asset purchases and direct lending by the treasury.* Governments and some central banks have provided substantial direct loans and have purchased illiquid assets from financial institutions. Amounts involved range widely, with such support in Canada, Japan, Norway, and the United Kingdom accounting for over 10 percent of GDP. The advanced G-20 average is $5\frac{1}{2}$ percent of GDP.

- *Guarantees for financial sector liabilities.* Guarantees have been provided for bank deposits, interbank loans and, in some cases, bonds. Deposit insurance limits have been raised in almost all countries. Guarantees provided in Ireland, the Netherlands, Sweden, and the United Kingdom are particularly large, relative to GDP.

- *Central bank support.* In addition to liquidity provided by expanding regular facilities, central bank support has been provided through credit lines to financial institutions, purchase of asset-backed securities and commercial paper, and asset swaps (see Appendix II).[5] In only a few countries have these operations been undertaken with upfront treasury financing (Table 2.1, column D shows the actual changes in central bank balance sheets since the beginning of the crisis).

While the support operations have been large, the immediate impact on financing needs has been more limited. The immediate impact averages $5\frac{1}{2}$ percent of GDP for the advanced G-20 (Table 2.1, last column). The figures are much larger when taking into account: (1) central bank liquidity provisions and (2) especially, guarantees, which do not require upfront financing.

---

[3]Some countries have also provided direct support to the nonfinancial sector but in fairly small amounts.

[4]In some instances, the amounts announced have not yet been formally committed through legislation or regulation (see Appendix II, Table A2.3 for details).

---

[5]For the euro area countries, the European Central Bank (ECB) has provided significant support since the summer of 2007, initially mainly through lengthening of the maturity of its refinancing operations, and since October 2008, through an increase in the aggregate amount of liquidity provision. This also applies to other major central banks, with some variation in the modalities in the provision of the support.

Box 2.1. Fiscal Accounting Treatment of Support to the Financial Sector
(Guidance based on Government Finance Statistics Manual (GFSM 2001))

The following is the recommended treatment of the impact on the government balance of the main financial support operations:

Capital grants. Increase the deficit by the amount of the grant.

Equity purchases. Have no impact on the fiscal balance, if purchase is at market value, but increase government gross debt. Raise the deficit by any marked/undisputable excess of what the government pays over the value of the equity.

Asset purchases/swaps. Same as equity purchases.

Loans. Have no immediate impact on the fiscal balance if there is no inherent subsidy, but increase government debt. Reduce the balance by any amount that the government cannot expect to be repaid.

Guarantees. Have no immediate impact on the fiscal balance or debt unless there is a significant probability the guarantee will be called (in practice, when a reserve has been created). In other cases, the fiscal balance would weaken and debt increase if and when the guarantee is called.

Associated fees, interest, and dividends. Affect the deficit in the same way as other government income or expense.

Central bank operations. Are reflected in its own balance sheet and income statement, rather than those of the government. However, losses on these operations will affect the budget over time, as they affect profit transfers or necessitate recapitalization. For transparency and to facilitate policy decision making, these operations should be disclosed, possibly as complementary information in the budget.

Emerging Markets

Financial sector support has been limited so far in emerging economies, which have only recently seen a pronounced impact of deleveraging and increased risk aversion on their financial sectors. The main measures announced include:[6]

- *Bank recapitalization.* Hungary, Poland, and Ukraine;

- *Liquidity provision.* Hungary, India, Mexico, Russia, Turkey, and Ukraine. These countries have extended (or committed to extend) liquidity facilities to banks or to state-owned or managed enterprises; and

- *Guarantees.* Blanket coverage has been provided in Egypt and Saudi Arabia; several other countries (Hungary, Indonesia, Mexico, Poland, and Russia) have committed to provide more limited guarantees (e.g., trade credit to exporters and interbank lending).

Based on the (limited) information available, the average immediate impact on gross debt of these operations is about ½ percent of GDP.

Net Cost over the Medium Term

The medium-term net budgetary cost of financial support operations will depend on the extent to which

the assets acquired by government or the central bank will hold their value and can be divested without losses, and the potential loss from guarantees. Although there are significant uncertainties relating to each of these channels, and the current crisis is unique in its complexity and pervasiveness, past experience can provide some guidance for asset recovery rates. Moreover, estimates of default probabilities based on financial market data can be used to provide an educated guess of the potential losses from guarantees.

Recovery Rates and Net Cost

The amounts recovered from the sale of assets acquired through interventions will likely vary significantly across countries, depending on the type of intervention, the approach followed in managing and selling the assets, and various macroeconomic factors. Econometric analysis suggests that recovery ratios are positively correlated with per capita income: advanced countries had higher recovery rates (an average of 51 percent compared with 13 percent for emerging markets—see Appendix III). Recovery rates are also higher, the stronger the fiscal balance at the start of the crisis, possibly an indicator of sounder fiscal and public financial management frameworks.

Based on these estimates, the medium-term impact on gross government debt could be substantially lower than the upfront impact, but still sizable. The average net cost for the G-20 advanced economies is projected to be 2½ percent of GDP, compared to upfront cost of 5½ percent of GDP (Appendix II, Table A2.1). In general, recovery rates estimated for emerging markets are

---

[6]Many countries noted below have announced measures that are difficult to quantify and so are not included in Table 2.1.

Table 2.1. Headline Support for Financial and Other Sectors and Upfront Financing Need
(As of June 2009; in percent of 2008 GDP; average using PPP GDP weights)[1]

	Capital Injection (A)	Purchase of Assets and Lending by Treasury[2] (B)	Guarantees[3] (C)	Liquidity Provision and Other Support by Central Bank (D)	Upfront Government Financing[4] (E)
Advanced North America					
Canada	0.0	10.9	13.5	1.5	10.9
United States	5.2	1.3	10.9	8.4	6.7[5]
Advanced Europe					
Austria	5.3	0.0	30.1	...	8.9
Belgium	4.8	0.0	26.4	...	4.8
France	1.4	1.3	16.4	...	1.6[6]
Germany	3.8	0.4	18.0	...	3.7
Greece	2.1	3.3	6.2	...	5.4
Ireland	5.9	0.0	198.1	...	5.9
Italy	0.7	0.0	0.0	...	0.7[7]
Netherlands	3.4	10.3	33.6	...	13.6
Norway	2.0	15.8	0.0	14.7	15.8[8]
Portugal	2.4	0.0	12.0	...	2.4[9]
Spain	0.0	4.6	18.3	...	4.6
Sweden	2.1	4.8	47.5	13.6	5.2[10]
Switzerland	1.1	0.0	0.0	25.5	1.1
United Kingdom	3.9	13.8	49.7	14.4	20.0[11]
European Central Bank (ECB)	...	...	...	6.4	...
Advanced Asia and Pacific					
Australia	0.0	0.7	8.8	...	0.7
Japan	2.4	21.2	7.3	2.9	0.8[12]
Korea	2.3	5.5	14.5	4.5	0.8[13]
Emerging economies					
Argentina	0.0	0.9	0.0	4.2	0.9[14]
Brazil	0.0	0.8	0.0	12.5	0.0[15]
China	0.0	0.0	0.0	21.3	0.0
India	0.4	0.0	0.0	9.2	0.4
Indonesia[16]	0.0	0.0	0.1	1.3	0.1
Hungary	1.1	2.4	1.1	15.7	3.5[17]
Poland	0.0	0.0	3.2	5.5	0.0
Russia	1.2	1.2	0.5	14.3	2.3
Saudi Arabia	0.0	1.2	N/A	33.1	1.2[18]
Turkey	0.0	0.3	0.0	3.1	0.0[19]
Average					
G-20	2.2	3.5	8.8	9.2	3.6
Advanced economies	3.4	5.4	14.0	6.8	5.6
In billions of U.S. dollars	1,149	1,946	4,646	2,484	1,858
Emerging economies	0.2	0.3	0.1	13.6	0.4
In billions of U.S. dollars	22	38	7	1,605	47

Sources: IMF staff estimates; and IMF, *World Economic Outlook*, April 2009. See Appendix II for details.

[1]Amounts in columns A, B, C, and E indicate announced or pledged amounts, and not actual uptake. Column D shows the actual changes in central bank's balance sheet from June 2007 to April 2009. While the expansion of central bank balance sheet is mostly related to measures aimed at enhancing market liquidity as well as financial sector support, it may occasionally have other causes. Also, it may not fully capture some other types of support, including those arising from changes in regulatory policies. For the euro area countries, see the ECB line. Averages for column D include the euro area as a whole.

[2]Column B does not include Treasury funds provided in support of central bank operations. These amount to 0.5 percent of GDP in the United States, and 12.8 percent in the United Kingdom.

[3]Excludes deposit insurance provided by deposit insurance agencies.

[4]This includes support measures that require upfront government outlays. It does not include recoveries from the sale of assets acquired through interventions.

[5]Estimated upfront financing need for 2009–10 is $960 billion (6.7 percent of GDP), consisting of the allocated amounts under the Troubled Asset Relief Program (TARP; $510 billion); Treasury purchases of government-sponsored enterprise preferred stocks ($400 billion); and Treasury support for Commercial Paper Funding Facility ($50 billion).

Table 2.1 (concluded)

[6]Support to the country's strategic companies is recorded under (B); of which €20 billion will be financed by a state-owned bank, Caisse des Dépôts et Consignations, not requiring upfront Treasury financing.

[7]It does not include the temporary swap of government securities for assets held by Italian banks undertaken by the Bank of Italy.

[8]Excluding asset accumulation in sovereign Wealth Fund, the balance sheet expansion during the period was only 4.5 percent of GDP.

[9]A maximum amount of €20 billion (12 percent of GDP) is allocated to both the guarantee scheme and the reinforcement of core capital, with the latter not exceeding €4 billion.

[10]Some capital injection (Skr 50 billion) will be undertaken by the Stabilization Fund.

[11]Estimated upfront financing need is £289 billion (20 percent of GDP), consisting of Bank Recapitalization Fund (£56 billion), Special Liquidity Scheme (£185 billion), and financing for the nationalization of Northern Rock and Bradford & Bingley (£48 billion).

[12]Budget provides ¥ 3,900 billion (0.8 percent of GDP) to support capital injection by a special corporation and lending and purchase of commercial paper by policy-based financing institutions.

[13]In 2009, W 8 trillion will be provided from the budget to support small and medium-sized enterprises (SMEs).

[14]IMF staff estimates.

[15]Liquidity support and loan purchases are provided through public banks and deposit insurance fund, and entail no upfront government financing.

[16]Small interventions have been recently implemented through the deposit insurance agency that are not yet quantified.

[17]The expansion of the central bank balance sheet reflects mostly the increase in net foreign assets as a result of IMF and European Union disbursements in the context of the Stand-By Arrangement. During this period, the increase in central bank domestic assets was limited to 2.3 percent of GDP.

[18]A significant part of the central bank balance sheet expansion was due to a large accumulation of foreign assets during 2008.

[19]Column B shows loans by the SME Industry Development Organization, not requiring direct Treasury financing.

markedly lower, so the difference between the gross and net outlays would be smaller.

The timing of asset recoveries will depend on the speed of the economic and financial recovery. Past experience indicates that the bulk of asset recovery takes place only after economic and financial recovery firms up demand and stabilizes asset prices. For example, Sweden achieved a recovery rate of 94 percent after only five years following the 1991 crisis, while Japan had recovered only 1 percent of assets after five years following the 1997 crisis (by 2008, the recovery rate for Japan reached 54 percent).

Net Cost of Central Bank Liquidity Support and of Government Guarantees

Potential costs involved in central bank liquidity support are likely to be more contained than those associated with government intervention. Given the unprecedented magnitude of central bank support operations, there is little evidence to assess likely recovery rates. However, in most countries, central banks have focused on providing liquidity support (with relatively short maturities and higher-quality collateral), whereas governments have generally provided solvency support—operations with the highest risk of loss. Therefore, the recovery rate for outlays by central banks is likely to be higher than for governments. Focusing on total commitments or announcements made through new special facilities (but excluding liquidity provision through regular facilities), the potential fiscal cost is illustrated in Appendix II. In some countries, actual disbursements have been significantly lower than the total announced facilities. The computation of net cost assumes recovery rates of

90 percent against the new facilities. Under these assumptions, the net cost from central bank operations could average $1\frac{3}{4}$ percent of GDP for advanced countries (Appendix II, Table A2.2).

The expected cost of the (explicit) guarantees provided so far is not trivial, but the margin of uncertainty is large. Some indicative estimates can be obtained using standard financial derivative pricing models—in particular, by estimating the expected default frequency implied credit default swap (EICDS) spreads and applying them to the guaranteed amounts. EICDS can be regarded as indicative of the "insurance" premium for providing the guarantees, and the approach—which takes into account market volatility and hence, the probability of default of individual institutions—provides an approximate measure of the cost to government of providing this "insurance." Based on November 2008 market data, outlays from contingent liabilities could be of the order of 1–3 percent of GDP (cumulative) for 2009–13 for the advanced G-20 countries, with a point estimate of $1\frac{3}{4}$ percent of GDP (Appendix II, Table A2.2). This range corresponds to the assumed recovery rates under an optimistic scenario (80 percent recovery rate) and a conservative scenario (40 percent recovery rate).[7]

---

[7]The point estimate reflects the EICDS spreads observed in the market. These spreads, once the guarantees are in place, capture the residual risk for banks, but may not capture the full risk for the government that is providing the guarantee. The approach, therefore, may bias downward the calculation of the potential costs for the government. To correct for this, a "conservative" CDS was calculated (assuming a conservative recovery rate—broadly in line with market practices) and used to derive the figure reported in the text as upper bound (see Appendix II, Table A2.2).

Potential Total Cost of Implicit and Explicit Guarantees

In case of additional market disturbances, governments may need to provide broader support than currently implied by the explicit guarantees. For illustrative purposes, it has been assumed that governments provide an implicit guarantee on all institutions that are systemic ("too big to fail"). To derive an estimate of the potential costs for governments arising from explicit and implicit guarantees, two approaches were followed. The first one is the approach noted in the previous paragraph, applied to all systemic institutions. The second one is the "contingent claim approach," applied to the same institutions (see Appendix IV for further details on both approaches). These approaches imply that the possible costs in case of further market disturbances could be of the order of 14–22 percent of GDP (cumulative for 2009–13) for the advanced countries, and 4–9 percent of GDP for the emerging economies in the sample (some of this financing, however, could come from the private sector).[8]

---

[8]These costs are calculated in Appendix IV, Table A4.1 (column A) and in Table A4.3 (column A), converted to a five-year measure.

III   Fiscal Implications of the Crisis: The Cost of the Recession

The recession (and actions to alleviate it) will involve fiscal costs through three channels: automatic stabilizers; other nondiscretionary effects going beyond the normal impact of the cycle, including from lower asset prices, financial sector profits, and commodity prices; and discretionary fiscal stimulus. Some of these effects will be short-lived; others will be longer lasting or even permanent. For example, the cyclical impact of automatic stabilizers will reverse with recovery, and some discretionary measures may explicitly incorporate sunset provisions. By contrast, tax breaks may be difficult to reverse, and while revenues associated with "normal" long-term trends in commodity and asset prices will resume, those associated with above-normal price levels before the crisis will not.

Automatic Stabilizers

The impact of the automatic stabilizers is increasing rapidly with the weakening of economic conditions.[9] For 2008, the estimated impact of automatic stabilizers—computed on the basis of changes in the output gap—is just –0.2 percent of GDP for the G-20. A larger impact, –1.8 percent of GDP, is projected in 2009, as the output gap widens (Table 3.1). The impact in 2009 ranges from –3.5 percent of GDP for Germany to –2½ percent for France, Italy, Japan, Russia, Turkey, and the United Kingdom, and to –½ percent for several emerging economies, including China, India, and Indonesia (differences across countries reflect differences in the change in the output gap and the revenue and expenditure elasticity assumptions). As a gauge for sensitivity analysis, a uniform 1 percentage point of GDP worsening in the G-20 output gap broadly translates into a ⅓ percent of GDP increase in the fiscal deficit. An intuition behind this approximation is that government size—a good proxy for the magnitude of automatic stabilizers—is around one-third of GDP for the G-20 weighted average.

Other Nondiscretionary Effects

Looking just at output gap changes is not sufficient to evaluate the effect of nondiscretionary factors on budgetary positions. In fact, some variables affecting fiscal balances are not perfectly correlated with output fluctuations. For example, exceptional declines in asset prices may reduce revenues by more than could be explained by looking at output gap changes. In quantifying these effects, however, it is important to avoid double-counting (i.e., the fact they would *partly* be captured by the standard output gap calculation).

Five effects are worth considering more closely:[10]

- *Equity prices.* Recent swings in equity prices were more pronounced than in past business cycles, and would, thus, not be fully included in the above estimates. The fall in revenues could come through several channels, including declines in capital gains taxation; a fall in wealth, consumption, and consumption tax revenue; and the impact on profit tax revenues from firms with trading activity. Staff regression estimates (see Appendix V) suggest that a 10 percent decline in equity prices leads cyclically adjusted revenues to fall by 0.07 and 0.08 percent of GDP in the current and subsequent years, close to estimates by Morris and Schuknecht (2007). Using these estimates, the equity market declines through end-2008 imply a cumulative fall in revenue for 2008–09 for the G-20 weighted average of 0.6 percent of GDP (of which 0.5 percent of GDP in 2009, assuming no further decline in equity prices takes place).

- *Housing prices.* Staff regression estimates suggest that a 10 percent decline in real housing prices leads to a 0.27 percent of GDP decline in cyclically adjusted revenues in the following year, a stronger elasticity than for equity price changes (see also Carroll, Otsuka, and Slacalek, 2006; and Morris and Schuknecht, 2007). However, as the decline

---

[9]See Appendix V for details on the computation of the automatic stabilizers. The estimates are based on noncommodity revenues.

[10]Severe disruptions in payment and credit markets could also abnormally reduce revenue collection, including through failure to file returns, underdeclaration, or payment deferrals. These effects, which may only affect the fiscal balance on a cash (and not accrual) basis, are difficult to estimate, and are not included here.

Table 3.1. G-20 Countries: Contribution of Automatic Stabilizers
(In percent of GDP, relative to previous year)[1]

	2008	2009
Automatic stabilizers	−0.2	−1.8
Of which:		
Advanced countries	−0.4	−2.1
Emerging market countries	0.1	−1.1

Sources: IMF, *World Economic Outlook*, April 2009; and IMF staff estimates.
[1]Averages, based on PPP GDP weights.

Table 3.2. Loss of Fiscal Revenue Due to Commodity Price Movements
(In percent of GDP)

	2008	2009
Argentina	0.0	−0.4
Australia	0.0	−0.4
Brazil	1.0	−2.8
Canada	0.3	−0.7
Indonesia	0.0	0.2
Mexico	0.8	−0.8
Russia	1.7	−5.9
Saudi Arabia	15.0	−29.7
South Africa	0.2	−0.1

Source: IMF staff estimates.

in housing prices has been smaller than for equity prices (less than 10 percent versus 50 percent), the fall in cyclically adjusted revenues arising from house price declines would be more contained (0.2 percent of GDP for the G-20 weighted average in 2009; see also Appendix V).

- *Financial sector profits.* In many countries, financial sector profits are an important source of corporate income tax (CIT) revenue; in some, stamp duties and financial transaction taxes are also levied. Over one-quarter of CIT revenues for the United States and the United Kingdom during 2000–07 came from the financial sector. Extrapolating from this, the decline in financial sector profits could contribute to a 0.2 percent of GDP additional revenue decline (evenly split between 2008 and 2009).[11]

- *Commodity prices.* The effect on fiscal revenues of the decline in commodity prices could be sizable in 2009 for some emerging markets (Table 3.2). For the G-20 group, the figures are smaller, but significant (0.7 percent of GDP in 2009), largely reflecting the impact on Russia, Saudi Arabia, and Brazil.[12] Some countries could benefit to the extent that governments decide not to pass through to users the

---

[11]CIT revenues averaged 3 percent of GDP across the G-20 during 2004–06 (weighted average). The calculation assumes that the financial sector pays 25 percent of CIT and has a decline in profits of 50 percent on top of the average decline in profits (already captured by the cyclical adjustment calculation). Because of the possible double-counting between this effect and the equity price effect, the former is reduced by a quarter.

[12]Another major G-20 oil producer, Mexico, hedged its 2009 oil export price at US$70 per barrel. Staff estimate that each 10 percent fall in commodity prices will reduce G-20 fiscal revenue by 0.15 percent of GDP.

Table 3.3. G-20 Countries: Other Nondiscretionary Factors
(In percent of GDP, relative to previous year)[1]

	2008			2009		
	All G-20	Advanced	Emerging	All G-20	Advanced	Emerging
Nondiscretionary factors	0.1	−0.4	1.0	−1.3	−0.5	−2.4
Equity prices	−0.2	−0.3	0.0	−0.5	−0.4	−0.5
Housing prices	0.1	−0.1	0.3	−0.2	−0.3	0.0
Financial sector	−0.1	−0.1	−0.2	−0.1	−0.1	−0.2
Interest payments	0.0	0.0	0.1	0.2	0.4	0.0
Commodity prices	0.3	0.0	0.8	−0.7	0.0	−1.8

Sources: IMF, *World Economic Outlook*, April 2009; Bloomberg and other financial sources (see Appendix V); and IMF staff estimates.
[1]Averages based on PPP GDP weights.

Table 3.4. G-20 Countries: Estimated Cost of Discretionary Measures
(In percent of GDP, relative to 2007 baseline)[1,2]

	2008	2009	2010
Argentina	0.0	1.5	...
Australia	1.2	2.5	2.1
Brazil	0.0	0.6	0.5
Canada	0.0	1.9	1.7
China	0.4	3.1	2.7
France	0.0	0.7	0.8
Germany	0.0	1.6	2.0
India[3,4]	0.6	0.6	0.6
Indonesia	0.0	1.4	0.6
Italy	0.0	0.2	0.1
Japan[5]	0.3	2.4	1.8
Korea	1.1	3.7	1.2
Mexico	0.0	1.5	...
Russia	0.0	4.1	1.3
Saudi Arabia	2.4	3.3	3.5
South Africa[3,6]	2.3	3.0	2.1
Spain[7]	1.9	2.3	...
Turkey[8]	0.0	0.8	0.3
United Kingdom	0.2	1.5	0.0
United States[9]	1.1	2.0	1.8
Total (PPP-weighted average)	0.6	2.0	1.5

Source: IMF staff estimates.

[1]Figures reflect the budgetary cost of crisis-related discretionary measures in each year compared to 2007 (baseline), based on measures announced through mid-May 2009. They do not include (1) "below-the-line" operations that involve acquisition of assets (including financial sector support) or (2) measures that were already planned for. Some figures represent staff's preliminary analysis.

[2]"..." is used for countries for which no information is available on the size of their fiscal packages.

[3]Fiscal year basis.

[4]Includes only on-budget measures. Additional off-budget measures amount to 0.8 percent of GDP in 2008/09 and 1.6 percent of GDP in 2009/10 (including 0.4 percent of GDP for bank recapitalization).

[5]Based on staff preliminary analysis, financial-sector-related measures of 0.1 percent of GDP in 2008, 0.5 percent of GDP in 2009, and 0.2 percent of GDP in 2010 are excluded. These measures cover both subsidies to and capital injections in public financial institutions.

[6]Based on staff estimates of the cyclically adjusted general government balance. Additional stimulus in the form of infrastructure investment is being provided by the broader public sector, so that the total fiscal stimulus (as measured by the public sector borrowing requirement) is 4.2 percent of GDP in 2008, 6.2 percent in 2009, and 4.9 percent in 2010.

[7]Budget liquidity impact basis.

[8]Includes only discretionary measures taken from September 2008 through March 2009. Another fiscal stimulus package was announced in early June, involving investment incentives, training, and short-term public sector employment. The impact of the package has not yet been quantified.

[9]Excludes cost of financial system support measures (estimated at 1.4 percent of GDP in 2008, 4.5 percent of GDP in 2009, and 0.9 percent of GDP in 2010).

decline in commodity prices. This decision—effectively a cut in subsidies or a tax increase—is considered a discretionary change, and associated fiscal savings are not included in these adjustments.

- *Interest rate and exchange rates.* In lower-risk countries, the decline in interest rates on government debt would reduce the debt service. In other countries, rising risk premia and exchange rate depreciation could raise it. However, the impact, in both directions, is likely to be modest in 2008 and 2009, at least in G-20 countries.

Overall, these other nondiscretionary effects appear to be sizable (Table 3.3). Their impact could account for an estimated 1.3 percent of GDP deterioration in fiscal positions of G-20 countries in 2009.

Discretionary Responses to the Crisis

Many countries have announced fiscal stimulus plans. On average, G-20 countries have adopted (or plan to adopt) stimulus measures amounting to ½ percent of GDP in 2008, 2.0 percent of GDP in

Table 3.5. G-20 Stimulus Measures, 2008–10[1]

Measure	Argentina	Australia	Brazil	Canada	China	France	Germany	India	Indonesia	Italy	Japan	Korea	Mexico	Russia	Saudi Arabia	South Africa	Spain	Turkey	United Kingdom	United States
Expenditure																				
Infrastructure investment		T		T	T	T	T	T	T	T	T	T	T		T	T	T		S	T
Support to SMEs and/or farmers			T	T	T	T		T	P	T	T	T	T	T		T	T	T	T	T
Safety nets			T	T	T	T	P	T	P	T	T	T	T	T		T	T		T	T
Housing/construction support		T		T		T	P	T		T	T	T		T			T		T	T
Strategic industries support			T		T	T	T	T		T		T					T	T	T	
Increase in public wage bill			T											T			T	T		
Other		T		T	T	T	T	T	T	T	T	T	T	T		T	T	T	T	T
Revenue																				
CIT/depreciation/incentives[2]		P		P	P	P	P	P	P	P	P	P		P		P	P	P	P	P
PIT/exemptions/deductions[3]			P	T	P			P	T	P	P	P		P			P	P	P	P
Indirect tax reductions/exemptions[4]	P	T		T	P	P		T	T	P	T						P	P	S	P
Other	P		T	T				P	P	P	T	T					T	P	P	P

Sources: Country authorities; and IMF staff estimates.

Note: T = temporary measures (with explicit sunset provisions or time-bound spending); S = self-reversing measures (measures whose costs are recouped by compensatory measures in future years); and P = permanent measures (with recurrent fiscal costs).

[1]Measures announced through early May 2009.

[2]Some of the corporate income tax (CIT) reductions in Germany, Italy, and Korea are temporary.

[3]Some of the personal income tax (PIT) reductions in Indonesia are temporary and some are self-reversing.

[4]The reduction in the value-added tax in the United Kingdom is a temporary measure, but lost revenue will be replaced by restricting personal income tax allowance and increasing income tax for high earners in 2010–11. For India and Italy, indirect tax reductions include a mix of permanent and temporary measures.

Figure 3.1. Composition of Discretionary Fiscal Measures in G-20 Countries, 2008–10
(Bubble size = percent of GDP; PPP-weighted average[1])

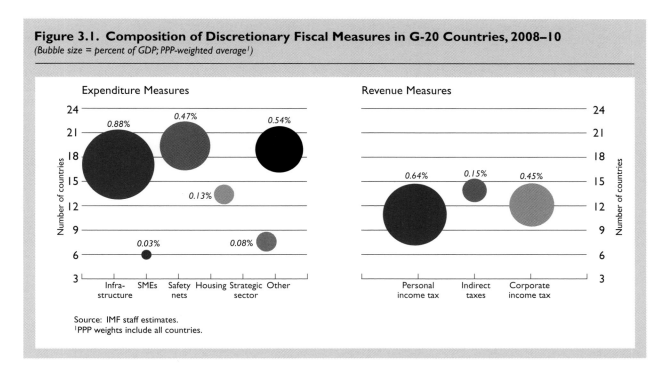

Source: IMF staff estimates.
[1]PPP weights include all countries.

2009, and 1.5 percent of GDP in 2010 (Table 3.4 and Appendix VI).[13]

The impact of these stimulus measures on government deficits and debts will vary, depending on their nature. Table 3.5 identifies three types of measures:

- *Temporary.* These measures will have a temporary effect on the deficit, but a permanent one on the debt level. Most of the stimulus measures on the spending side are designed to expire after a certain period (although some spending programs may have recurrent cost implications, such as maintenance costs for new infrastructure projects).

- *Permanent.* These measures have a permanent effect on the deficit, and a cumulative one on debt. Most revenue measures announced so far are permanent.

- *Self-reversing.* These have a temporary effect on both deficit and debt. Few measures are truly self-reversing (e.g., bringing forward some investment spending). But some *sets of measures*, as a whole, could have no long-term impact. For example, in the United Kingdom, the upfront value-added tax (VAT) cut will be offset by revenue-increasing measures starting in 2010.

[13]These figures reflect the budgetary cost of the stimulus measures in each year. They are based on packages announced through mid-May 2009. The figures have been corrected for (1) "below-the-line" operations that do not have an impact on the fiscal balance; and (2) the fact that in some countries part of the announced stimulus included measures that were already planned before the crisis.

Almost two-thirds of the fiscal stimulus has so far been represented by expenditure measures with particular emphasis on increased spending for infrastructure (see Figure 3.1 and Table 3.5).

- Seventeen of the G-20 countries have announced plans to increase spending on infrastructure, many on transportation networks (Australia, Canada, France, Germany, Korea, and Saudi Arabia, among others)—either in the form of direct central government spending, or through capital transfers to local authorities.

- Several countries have announced plans to protect vulnerable groups, including by strengthening unemployment benefits (Canada, Russia, Turkey, the United Kingdom, and the United States), cash transfers to the poor (Korea), or support to children (Australia and Germany) or pensioners (Australia and Canada).

- A few G-20 countries are also stepping up support for small and medium-sized enterprises (SMEs; e.g., Korea) and strategic or vulnerable sectors, such as forestry and construction (in Canada and in Germany, for energy efficient buildings and repairs and renovations) and defense and agriculture (Russia).

- Finally, a few countries are using stimulus measures to address longer-term policy challenges, such as improving the quality of health and education (Australia, China, and Saudi Arabia) or introducing incentives for environmentally friendly technologies (China, Germany, and the United Kingdom).

Revenue measures—in terms of relative magnitude—have targeted primarily households, through cuts in personal income and indirect taxes.

- Fourteen G-20 countries have announced sizable cuts in personal income taxes (including Brazil, Canada, Germany, Indonesia, Japan, Spain, the United Kingdom, and the United States); while in six, indirect tax cuts have been announced.

- Cuts in the CIT have also been frequent but not as large; these include outright reduction in the CIT rate (Canada, Korea, and Russia), investment incentives (France and Korea), or more favorable depreciation schedules (Germany, Russia, and the United States).

IV Fiscal Implications of the Crisis: Effects Through the Funded Component of the Pension System

A key fiscal risk presented by the crisis is its effect on funded components of the pension system, both public and private. The level of funding for pensions has increased rapidly in recent years as a share of GDP, reflecting both earnings on existing retirement saving and net deposits (Figure 4.1). Some of the countries most affected by the recent stock market decline are those where private pensions play an important role in mandatory pension provision. It is useful to assess at the outset the overall loss suffered by funded pension schemes.

Losses of Funded Pension Schemes

Public and private pension fund losses are concentrated in a limited number of countries. These are countries that, with more mature funded pension schemes, have higher shares of equities and mutual funds in pension fund portfolios and higher shares of pension saving in relation to GDP:[14] 16 of the 46 countries for which data are available have pension fund investments in equities and mutual funds greater than 10 percent of GDP (brown circles in Figure 4.2). Countries more exposed include Australia, the United States, Canada, Iceland, the Netherlands, Switzerland, Denmark, and the United Kingdom. Among emerging economies, South Africa, Chile, and Brazil are more exposed. Estimated losses in the United States and the United Kingdom during 2008 are, respectively, 22 percent and 31 percent of GDP.

A separate risk is pension fund exposure to potentially "toxic" assets, such as mortgage-backed securities and credit default swaps. The OECD has estimated average holdings of 3 percent of such assets in the portfolios of pension funds of member countries (OECD, 2008). Structured products—the class of assets within which toxic assets fall—represent about 8 percent of pension fund assets worldwide. The risk is concentrated in the United States, Sweden, and Japan.

---

[14]Mutual funds in these countries are also heavily weighted toward equities. Investment by funded pension funds in real estate is small (below 3 percent of total assets, on average, for member countries of the Organization for Economic Cooperation and Development (OECD)).

Risks for Fiscal Accounts

The risks for governments are difficult to quantify exactly, but are significant. They stem from (1) direct effects arising from investments by government pension funds in assets affected by the crisis; (2) explicit guarantees provided by governments to funded schemes; and (3) pressures to make up for losses suffered by pensioners covered by private pension plans. Whether these risks will materialize depends on the timing and the extent of the recovery in asset prices.

Direct effects relate to

- Pension plans sponsored by governments for their employees, which are significant in some countries. For example, as of end-2007, over $4 trillion of assets were held by federal, state, and local government defined-benefit pension plans in the United States (more than one-fifth of total U.S. pension assets). The value of these assets had fallen by roughly $1 trillion by October 2008 (Munnell, Aubry, and Muldoon, 2008). Three-quarters of these assets are held by state and local pension plans, which are typically subject to stringent funding requirements. The drop in equity prices will trigger requirements to close the resulting funding gap over the next five years (on a mark-to-market basis, the estimated aggregate funding ratio fell to 65 percent in October 2008). During 2000–02, when the equity market experienced a similarly sharp decline, contributions subsequently increased by 45 percent over a two-year period. Although contributions are presently shared between the employer and employees, recent court rulings in some states and restrictions on modifying accrued pension benefits imply that the burden of making up the current shortfall is likely to fall primarily on employers and, indirectly, on taxpayers.

- National social insurance pension plans—these also hold significant assets affected by the crisis. In some countries (e.g., the United States), these assets are specialized and largely impervious to financial market movements. In other countries (e.g., Japan, Canada, the Netherlands, and New

Figure 4.1. Pension Fund Assets in OECD Countries
(End-year 1995 to end-year 2007)

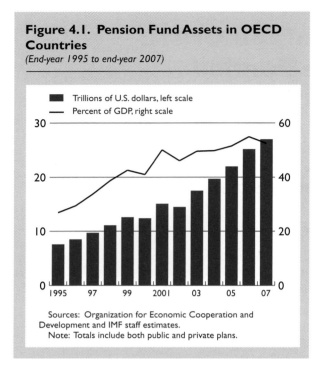

Sources: Organization for Economic Cooperation and Development and IMF staff estimates.
Note: Totals include both public and private plans.

Zealand), national pension systems hold a substantial quantity of marketable securities, including equities. However, national pension systems are not typically fully funded, and the impact may be postponed or mitigated by recovery.

Figure 4.2. Pension Plan Assets by Economy, End-2007

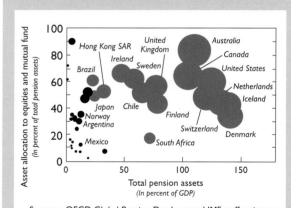

Sources: OECD Global Pension Database; and IMF staff estimates.
Note: Size of circles represents pension funds' equity and mutual fund assets as a percent of GDP. Brown circles denote countries where this value exceeds 10 percent of GDP. Data do not include reserve funds of social security systems of funds whose assets may be used for purposes other than financing the social security system, such as in Norway.

Explicit guarantees have been provided in two forms:

- Insurance against the loss of assets in private, defined-benefit plans due to employer insolvency (Canada (province of Ontario), Germany, Japan, Sweden, Switzerland, the United Kingdom, and the United States). Maximum benefits differ across countries, with the United States, the United Kingdom, Sweden, and Germany offering relatively high amounts. The crisis has yet to lead to widespread claims on these schemes; however, it is possible that the shock may overwhelm those already in deficit and require government intervention.[15] In the United States, the federal Pension Benefit Guaranty Corporation (PBGC), represents a sizable potential liability to the federal government, although legislation would be necessary for this liability to be significant. In the United Kingdom, the Pension Protection Fund (PPF) is not explicitly backed by taxpayers, but should the balance on these schemes deteriorate further, pressures for government financial support may arise. Recent estimates suggest that potential costs to the government arising from deficits of the guarantee funds as well as from contingent liabilities of probable employer bankruptcies would amount to 0.4 percent of GDP in the United States and 0.1 percent of GDP in the United Kingdom (PBGC, 2008; and PPF, 2008). These costs will likely increase if economic conditions deteriorate further.

- Guarantees of minimum benefits or rates of return for defined-contribution pension plans (France, Spain, Switzerland, the United Kingdom, and many Eastern European countries) (Whitehouse, 2007).

Arguably the largest fiscal risk is that the government may be forced to step in to support participants covered by private pension plans severely hit by the crisis.[16] This could happen for

- "Unprotected" defined-contribution plans (roughly three-quarters of defined-contribution assets). Younger workers may wait for market recovery. Older workers are likely to suffer more severe cuts in retirement income, particularly those who have to purchase annuities. The depressed value in their accounts, combined with low interest rates, will make the purchase of annuities less favorable.

---

[15]Partly because of low pricing of premiums, weak funding rules, and limited adjustment for plan-sponsor risk, guarantee schemes in the United States, the United Kingdom, and Ontario, Canada were in deficit in 2008.

[16]In the United States, pension plans of S&P 1500 companies lost nearly half a trillion dollars in 2008, nearly 80 percent of which occurred in the last quarter (Mercer, 2009).

- Defined-benefit plans run by private employers where benefits can be cut under certain conditions. Funding rules determine the extent and timing of increases in contributions and the degree to which benefits can be reduced.[17]

---

[17]To avert windup of plans, there are increasing demands for temporarily amending funding rules. Several countries are considering regulatory adjustments, for example, to adjust the time within which pension plans have to restore adequate funding levels. For example, in December 2008, the U.S. Congress rolled back part of the Pension Protection Act of 2006, which had increased the funding requirements of underfunded plans. Concerns remain, however, that such a relaxation would weaken the long-term health of the plans, affecting members and the government in the future.

To some extent, the potential call for government support will be influenced by the distributional incidence of the losses of participants in these plans. Among people over age 65 in the United States, for instance, funded pensions and annuities account for 21 percent of income of the richest income quintile, but just 3 percent for the poorest (Burtless, 2009). In the United Kingdom, occupational pensions comprise over 30 percent of income for the richest quintile of pensioners and only 1 percent for the poorest. In a few countries, however, funded plans cover a larger share of the retirement income of lower-income pensioners. For instance, all participants in the Chilean pension system invest in individual accounts, although the government does guarantee a minimum pension level.

V The Outlook for Public Finances in Light of the Crisis

This section assesses the short- and medium-term outlook for public finances, bringing together the themes discussed in earlier sections. There is, of course, considerable uncertainty around this outlook, and outcomes could be significantly worse than the baseline figures reported below in case of further distress and weaker output growth.[18]

Short-Term Outlook

Fiscal balances will be severely affected by the crisis in the short run. For G-20 advanced economies, fiscal balances are projected to worsen, on average, by 8 percentage points of GDP in 2009 relative to 2007 (see Table 5.1), thus reaching 9¾ percent of GDP in 2009 (Figure 5.1). The fiscal balances of G-20 emerging economies deteriorate less—given the lower impact on growth, automatic stabilizers, and fiscal stimulus—but still significantly (reversing the improvement achieved

---

[18]Baseline data are from the IMF's April 2009 *World Economic Outlook*.

since 2003). For the advanced countries, half of the deterioration is due to fiscal stimulus and financial sector support, while for emerging economies, a relatively large component is due to declining commodity and asset prices (Figure 5.2).

The increase in government debt ratios will be even more sizable (Figure 5.1). The debt-to-GDP ratio of advanced countries is expected to rise by 20 percentage points over 2008–09, the most pronounced upturn in the last few decades (Figure 5.3). The one-year increase in government debt in 2009 is three times as large as that experienced during the 1993 recession. More than a quarter of this increase is due to financial sector support packages. The debt ratio for the average of the emerging economies also shows a sizable increase in 2009, the first since 2002.

The Medium-Term Outlook and Risk Assessment

In the medium term, fiscal balances are expected to improve, while remaining weaker than before the

Table 5.1. G-20 Countries: Change in Fiscal Balances and Government Debt[1]

(In percent of GDP, difference with respect to previous period)

	2008 (A)	2009 (B)	2008–09 (A + B)
Fiscal balance			
Advanced G-20 countries	−2.5	−5.5	−8.0
Emerging market G-20 countries	−0.6	−4.5	−5.1
G-20 countries	−1.8	−5.1	−6.9
Public debt			
Advanced G-20 countries	5.8	14.2	20.0
Emerging market G-20 countries	−1.3	2.3	0.9
G-20 countries	3.1	9.8	12.9

Source: IMF, *World Economic Outlook (WEO)*, April 2009.

[1]General government if available, otherwise most comprehensive fiscal aggregate reported in the *WEO*. Table reports PPP GDP-weighted averages.

Figure 5.1. G-20 Countries: Outlook for Public Finances[1]
(In percent of GDP)

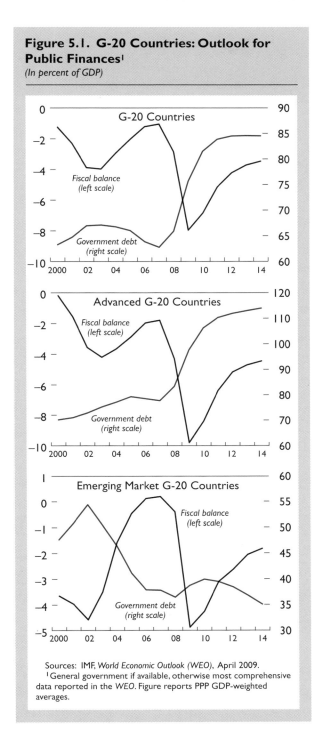

Sources: IMF, *World Economic Outlook (WEO)*, April 2009.
[1] General government if available, otherwise most comprehensive data reported in the *WEO*. Figure reports PPP GDP-weighted averages.

Figure 5.2. Impact of the Crisis on Public Finances: Contributing Factors[1]
(In percent of GDP)

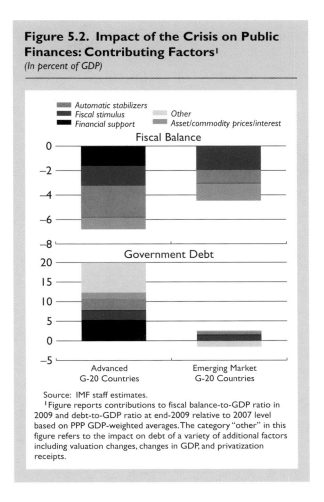

Source: IMF staff estimates.
[1] Figure reports contributions to fiscal balance-to-GDP ratio in 2009 and debt-to-GDP ratio at end-2009 relative to 2007 level based on PPP GDP-weighted averages. The category "other" in this figure refers to the impact on debt of a variety of additional factors including valuation changes, changes in GDP, and privatization receipts.

Nevertheless, unless tightening measures are introduced later, fiscal balances for advanced economies would remain weaker in the medium term than in 2007. Moreover, also for advanced economies, the effect on debt ratios would be long lasting: the debt-to-GDP ratio in 2014 is projected to be 36 percentage points above the 2007 level (Table 5.2).[19] For emerging economies, the projected medium-term debt path is more benign owing to higher growth. Still, debt ratios in 2010 will be above their 2007 levels, and the declining trend will not resume until 2011.

It is worth stress-testing these projections for more pessimistic assumptions. Two scenarios are explored:

- *Lower growth in 2009–11.* If growth is 1 percent a year below the baseline during 2009–11, fiscal deficits would rise, on average, by 1 percent of GDP, and the debt-to-GDP ratio would increase by

---

[19]These projections assume different recovery rates for the financial support operations as discussed in Section II, depending on the nature of the support.

crisis. Beyond 2009, activity is expected to recover, reflecting supportive macroeconomic and financial sector policies. Fiscal balances are projected to improve (Figure 5.1 and Table 5.2) as some of the stimulus measures are temporary and as the effects of the automatic stabilizers are gradually reversed.

Figure 5.3. G-20 Advanced Countries: Evolution of Government Debt[1]
(In percent of GDP)

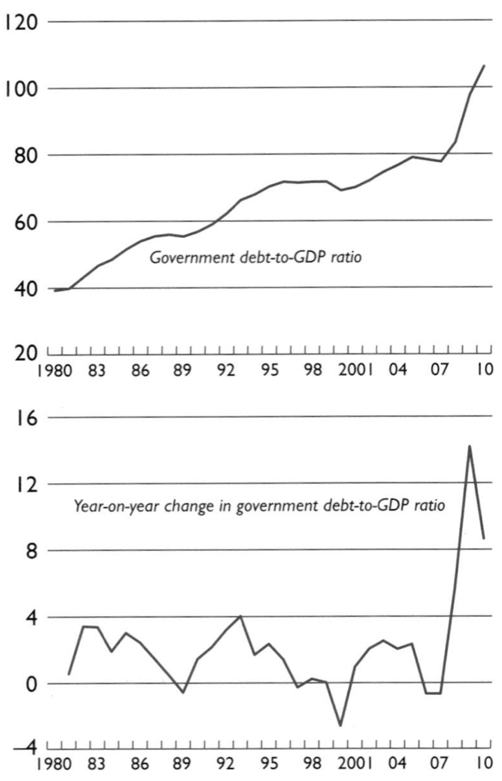

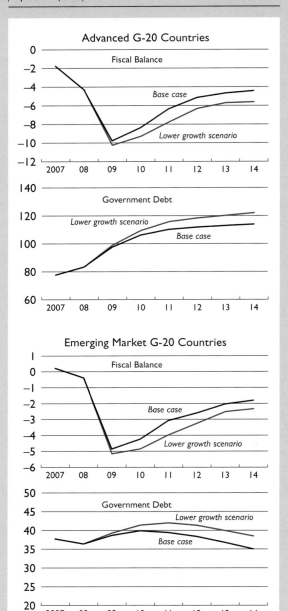

Figure 5.4. Lower Growth Scenario[1]
(In percent of GDP)

Source: IMF, *World Economic Outlook (WEO)*, April 2009.
[1] Averages based on PPP GDP weights.

Source: IMF staff estimates.
[1] Figure reports results of a 1 percentage point decline in growth relative to baseline during 2009–11.

an additional 6 percentage points by 2011 (Figure 5.4). This deterioration would mainly reflect the automatic stabilizers. Fiscal balances in emerging economies are less adversely affected, mainly because of their smaller automatic stabilizers (but could be affected more significantly through further declines in commodity prices).

- *A prolonged stagnation.* What would be the effect of a protracted deflationary slump, akin to the experience of Japan in the 1990s? From 1991 to 2007, GDP annual growth in Japan averaged 1.6 percent, a drop of 2.3 percentage points compared with the 1970–90 average. In light of that experience, a decline in growth (relative to the baseline) of 2 percentage points during 2009–13—was investigated. In this scenario, for the advanced countries, fiscal balances would deteriorate, on

Table 5.2. Public Finances[1,2]
(In percent of GDP)

	Fiscal Balance					
	2006	2007	2008	2009	2010	2014
Argentina	−1.1	−2.0	−0.5	−3.3	−2.8	−1.7
Australia	1.9	1.5	−0.7	−4.3	−5.3	−2.0
Brazil	−2.9	−2.2	−1.5	−1.9	−0.8	−0.6
Canada	1.3	1.4	0.4	−3.4	−3.6	0.4
China	−0.7	0.9	−0.3	−3.6	−3.6	−0.2
France	−2.4	−2.7	−3.4	−6.2	−6.5	−4.6
Germany	−1.5	−0.5	−0.1	−4.7	−6.1	−1.4
India	−5.7	−5.2	−8.4	−10.2	−8.7	−4.7
Indonesia	0.2	−1.2	0.0	−2.5	−2.2	−1.7
Italy	−3.3	−1.5	−2.7	−5.4	−5.9	−4.5
Japan	−4.0	−2.5	−5.6	−9.9	−9.8	−7.1
Korea	1.7	3.5	1.1	−3.2	−4.7	0.0
Mexico	−0.6	−1.4	−1.8	−3.6	−3.7	−2.7
Russia	8.3	6.8	4.3	−6.2	−5.0	−4.4
Saudi Arabia	24.6	15.8	35.5	−3.8	−1.4	5.8
South Africa	0.8	1.2	−0.4	−2.9	−3.2	−2.3
Spain	2.0	2.2	−3.8	−7.5	−7.5	−4.0
Turkey	−0.7	−2.1	−2.7	−5.9	−5.1	−3.6
United Kingdom	−2.6	−2.6	−5.4	−9.8	−10.9	−6.4
United States	−2.2	−2.9	−6.1	−13.6	−9.7	−4.7
G-20 countries	−1.2	−1.0	−2.8	−8.0	−6.9	−3.4
Advanced G-20 countries	−1.9	−1.8	−4.3	−9.8	−8.4	−4.4
Emerging market G-20 countries	0.1	0.2	−0.4	−4.8	−4.2	−1.8

	Government Debt					
	2006	2007	2008	2009	2010	2014
Argentina	76.5	67.9	57.7	50.4	50.6	48.5
Australia	9.6	8.9	8.9	11.3	13.9	16.6
Brazil	63.7	67.7	64.5	65.4	64.0	54.1
Canada	67.9	64.2	63.6	75.4	77.2	66.2
China	16.5	20.2	17.7	19.8	21.6	17.9
France	63.6	63.9	67.3	74.9	80.3	89.7
Germany	66.0	63.6	67.2	79.4	86.6	91.0
India	82.2	80.4	81.9	86.8	88.9	76.8
Indonesia	39.0	35.1	32.3	32.9	32.8	31.0
Italy	106.5	103.5	105.8	115.3	121.1	129.4
Japan	191.3	187.7	196.3	217.2	227.4	234.2
Korea	34.1	33.0	33.6	40.0	46.3	51.8
Mexico	38.3	38.2	43.3	46.9	49.3	44.0
Russia	9.1	7.3	5.8	6.9	7.0	7.4
Saudi Arabia	27.3	18.7	15.8	15.6	13.1	7.9
South Africa	33.0	28.5	27.3	29.1	30.8	29.9
Spain	39.6	36.2	39.4	51.8	59.2	69.2
Turkey[3]	46.1	39.4	39.5	47.2	50.4	53.7
United Kingdom	43.3	44.1	51.9	62.7	72.7	87.8
United States	61.9	63.1	70.5	87.0	97.5	106.7
G-20 countries	63.1	62.8	65.9	75.6	81.5	84.5
Advanced G-20 countries	78.3	77.6	83.4	97.6	106.2	114.0
Emerging market G-20 countries	37.6	37.8	36.4	38.7	39.9	35.0

Source: IMF, *World Economic Outlook (WEO)*, April 2009.
[1]The fiscal balance corresponds to general government if available, otherwise most comprehensive fiscal balance reported in the *WEO*.
[2]Averages based on PPP GDP weights.
[3]Fiscal projections reflect IMF staff estimates based on the authorities' policy intentions as stated in the EU Pre-Accession Program document.

Figure 5.5. Prolonged Slowdown Secenario[1]
(In percent of GDP)

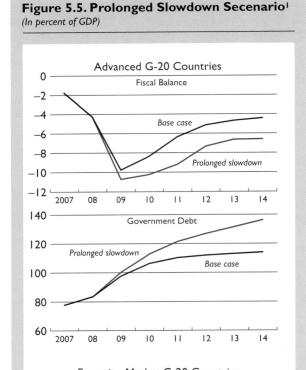

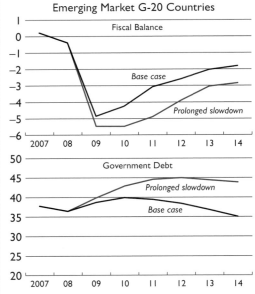

Source: IMF staff estimates.
[1] Figure reports results of a 2 percentage point decline in growth relative to baseline starting in 2009. Averages based on PPP GDP weights.

Figure 5.6. Government Debt in Case of Prolonged Slowdown, Higher Interest Rate, and Contingent Liability Shock[1]
(In percent of GDP)

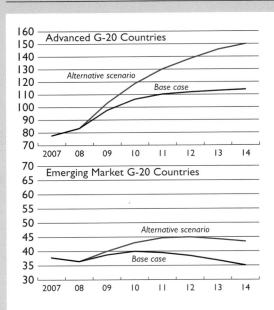

Source: IMF staff estimates.
[1] Figure reports results of a 2 percentage point decline in growth and a 200 basis point increase in real interest rates relative to the baseline starting in 2009, as well as a contingent liability shock corresponding to expected cost of guarantees (column A in Table A4.1 in Appendix IV). Averages based on PPP GDP weights.

average by 2 percentage points of GDP relative to the baseline, with debt ratios rising by 18 percentage points by 2013 (Figure 5.5). The deterioration is also notable for emerging economies.

There are other significant downside risks.

- Because of the considerable margin of uncertainty, the baseline estimates do not take into account the potentially large contingent liabilities of the government arising from explicit and implicit guarantees and central bank support operations. These additional costs could materialize in case of further financial instability, and further raise government debt in advanced countries (see the section "Net Cost of Central Bank Liquidity Support and of Government Guarantees").

- Government intervention to support financial markets has so far been limited in emerging market countries. However, the ramifications of the crisis in these countries may not have yet been fully felt, and stronger government support may be needed.

- The recovery rates assumed in the baseline may not materialize. Recovery rates in the aftermath of this global crisis could be particularly low, for example, because of the dearth of external buyers and increased risk aversion.

- The baseline does not include the possible costs arising from the support that the public sector may be called to provide to fully funded pension schemes. As discussed in Section IV, these costs could be significant.

- What makes things worse is that these additional risks are not independent from those aris-

ing from the shocks discussed in the previous paragraph. Indeed, they are more likely to arise in the context of weaker output growth. They could also be accompanied by heightened concerns about fiscal solvency, leading to higher interest rates. All these risks could materialize at the same time, with a major deterioration of the fiscal outlook with respect to an already weak baseline (Figure 5.6), and at a time when supportive fiscal action may, in principle, still be needed.

VI The Risk for Fiscal Solvency and the Appropriate Policy Response

The deterioration of the fiscal outlook highlighted in Section V raises issues of fiscal solvency, and could eventually trigger adverse market reactions. Doubts about fiscal solvency—the risk that governments find it more convenient to repudiate their debt or to inflate it away—could lead to an increase in the cost of borrowing. In turn, higher interest rates (and exchange rate depreciations in countries with significant borrowing in foreign currency, like most emerging economies) could further add to government debts—in some cases, resulting in "snowballing" debt dynamics. This scenario would be deleterious for global growth. Indeed, economic agents' confidence in governments' solvency has been a source of stability and has, so far, helped to avoid a complete meltdown of financial markets.

Thus far, government debt market reaction to the weaker fiscal outlook has been relatively muted, but not all signs are reassuring. Long-term nominal interest rates have declined in the main advanced economies since the beginning of the crisis (Figure 6.1). However:

- Real interest rates are broadly the same as in early 2007 (where these can be reliably observed from long-term inflation-indexed bonds traded on liquid markets, for example, in the United States and the United Kingdom),[20] although one might have expected a decline as a result of cyclical developments.

- For some highly indebted advanced economies (e.g., Greece and Italy), spreads have risen significantly, although government bond yields in those countries remain broadly similar to their precrisis levels (Figure 6.1).[21]

- There has been an uptick in credit default swap (CDS) spreads in recent months for some of the major advanced countries, including the United States, though the implied perceived default risk remains relatively small.[22]

- Sovereign bond spreads for emerging economies have risen sharply—reflecting increased risk aversion, and far in excess of what would seem warranted on the basis of domestic fundamentals. The EMBI Global composite spread rose to 750 basis points in December 2008 from 170 basis points in the beginning of 2007, and primary bond issuance slowed sharply—issuance by all emerging markets in August–December 2008 was half of its level during the same period in 2007.

More generally, recent history suggests that an abrupt market reaction to weakening fundamentals is possible. Thus, it is necessary to look closely at the risks arising from the deterioration of the fiscal outlook, and to draw implications for fiscal policy in the medium term.

The Level of Government Debt

The rise in government debt levels caused by the crisis does not, in itself, have major adverse implications for solvency:

- Fiscal solvency requires that government debt is not on an explosive path (as this would violate the government's intertemporal budget constraint—that is, the no-Ponzi-game condition that the government does not borrow just to pay interest on debt).[23] Following the simple arithmetic of changes in the debt-to-GDP ratio (Box 6.1), a one-off rise in the government debt ratio only requires

---

[20]This trend is also confirmed for other advanced countries using consensus inflation forecasts to estimate real bond yields.

[21]Spreads also rose to above 200 basis points for Ireland (Figure 6.1), where government guarantees provided to financial sector obligations amount to about 200 percent of GDP.

[22]CDS spreads for the United States rose from 8 basis points in June 2008 to almost 100 basis points in late February 2009 before moderating to around 50 basis points by mid-April 2009. Similarly, CDS spreads for Austria, Greece, Iceland, Ireland, Italy, Portugal, and Spain had all risen more than 150 basis points (by end-February 2009, compared with their June 2008 levels), though in some cases they declined somewhat by mid-April 2009.

[23]Strictly speaking, the no-Ponzi-game condition is equivalent to the stabilization of the debt-to-GDP ratio only if the interest rate on government debt exceeds the growth rate of the economy (otherwise, it is more stringent). It is, however, common to assume that this is the case in the long run.

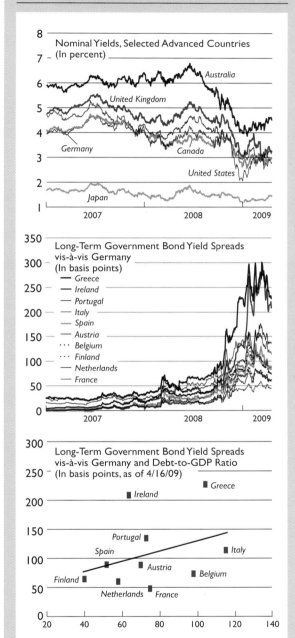

Figure 6.1. Long-Term Government Bond Yields and Spreads

Sources: IMF, World Economic Outlook database; Bloomberg; and IMF staff calculations.

Note: 10-year government bonds. Nominal yields in the top panel; spreads vis-à-vis Germany in the middle and bottom panels. In the bottom panel, the slope coefficient is 1.3 (i.e., a 10 percentage point increase in the debt-to-GDP ratio is associated with a 13 basis point increase in spreads).

a small increase in the primary balance to ensure solvency: for example, a rise in the government debt-to-GDP ratio by 10 percentage points requires an improvement in the primary balance of less than 0.1 percentage point of GDP to stabilize the debt ratio (assuming an interest rate/growth differential of 1 percentage point, in line with the average of the past few decades).

- The rise in government debt observed so far in advanced countries, while sizable, is not exceptional from a long-term perspective. Historically, large debt accumulations (bringing the debt to 100–200 percent of GDP) have resulted from war-related spending, prolonged recessions, or protracted fiscal problems (Table 6.1 and Figure 6.2).

- Highly disruptive ways of reducing debt/GDP ratios have occurred in some instances, but not since the 1940s for advanced countries.[24]

- A rise in debt ratios does not seem likely, in itself, to cause a large increase in interest rates. While such an increase would make the solvency arithmetic less favorable, empirical evidence shows that, in normal circumstances and in advanced countries, even a 10 percentage point of GDP increase in debt ratios would raise interest rates only by a few basis points (at least, if debt ratios are below 100 percent). (See Appendix VII.)

However, the rise in government debt cannot be ignored:

- There is a need to avoid the perception that all one-off shifts in debt ratios would be accommodated: in order to allow government debt to act as shock absorber in bad years, it must improve in good years. Thus, particularly in countries with relatively high debt ratios, it will be necessary not just to *stabilize* the debt ratio but to bring it back to its precrisis level (or even below, if the initial level was excessive). In this respect, in 2014, gross government debt ratios would stand above 100 percent of GDP in six advanced economies (Belgium, Greece, Ireland, Italy, Japan, and the United States) and between 60–100 percent of GDP in ten (Table 6.2).[25] This level of debt sets

---

[24]Hyperinflations occurred in the aftermath of major wars and in a context of domestic political instability, although moderate inflation has also occasionally played a significant role in reducing the real value of debt—especially until the 1950s. Partial defaults occurred during the interwar period, for example, in Italy in the late 1920s (Alesina, 1988), and in the United States in 1933, when the abrogation of "gold clauses" in debt contracts prevented a 25 percentage point increase in the government debt/GDP ratio (Kroszner, 2003).

[25]Some advanced countries have exhibited strong resilience to high government debt. Japan is the most noteworthy example. See Appendix VIII for a discussion of the idiosyncratic reasons that may explain such resilience.

Box 6.1. Debt/GDP Stabilizing Primary Balance

$$\Delta\left(\frac{D}{Y}\right)_t = \left(\frac{r-g}{1+g}\right)\left(\frac{D}{Y}\right)_{t-1} - pb$$

where D is the debt stock, Y is GDP, r is the nominal interest rate, g is the nominal growth rate, pb is the primary fiscal balance as a share of GDP, and Δ indicates a change over the previous year. The debt ratio is constant when $pb = (D/Y)(r-g)/(1+g)$.

a more demanding requirement on the primary balance: for example, for a 10 percent increase in the debt ratio, the primary balance would have to improve by more than 1 percentage point to bring back the ratio to its original level within 10 years.

- Debt tolerance seems to be lower for emerging economies. Indeed, government debt was below 60 percent of GDP in most default cases recorded in emerging economies in recent decades, though there has been wide variation (Reinhart, Rogoff, and Savastano, 2003; and IMF, 2003). Lower debt tolerance in these countries may reflect factors related to liquidity and solvency risks, such as greater reliance on financing by nonresidents; low shares of long-term, domestic currency denominated debt; and low and volatile revenue-to-GDP ratios.

- Rollover risks are likely to increase. Market analysts have recently focused on increased debt issuance by advanced countries in 2009. While roll-over risk has in the past been seen as affecting primarily emerging economies, higher-debt advanced countries may also be more exposed in coming years.

- When considering lessons from history, it is important to bear in mind two important differences. First, in wartime episodes, debt financing was facilitated by comprehensive government control over the economy, including capital controls. Moreover, citizens may feel the "moral duty" to support the war effort by purchasing government debt. Second, the current crisis involves truly novel features compared with historical episodes: in particular, it involves large contingent liabilities associated with guarantees of financial sector obligations; and it takes place, in many countries, in a context where pension and health care systems will give rise to large future spending increases. We turn to these factors in the next section.

The Dynamics of Government Debt: Current and Future Deficits

Debt solvency is a forward-looking concept. Public debt dynamics are driven not only by current but also future deficits. As discussed earlier, the crisis has led to a weakening of fiscal flows, not just stocks.

Primary balances, in particular, are now at levels that, in many countries, are insufficient to ensure debt stabilization, let alone to reduce debt to precrisis levels. For some of the main advanced countries where the crisis has resulted in large increases in debt—including the United Kingdom and the United States—the primary fiscal balance would have to improve, starting in 2014, by a few percentage points of GDP (compared with "unchanged policies" projections) to gradually bring the debt back to, say, 60 percent of GDP over the following 15 years (Table 6.2). More generally, almost all the advanced countries reported in Table 6.2 will still have primary balances in 2014 that are below what is required to stabilize their government debts (or bring them gradually down to 60 percent), in spite of the projected cyclical recovery of output and revenues (assuming an interest rate/growth rate differential of 1 percent). For a sample of selected emerging markets, the share of countries with 2014 primary balances below the level needed to stabilize the debt ratio or reduce it to a benchmark level of 40 percent of GDP is lower, but still more than one-half. Primary gaps would be larger if the risks to the baseline materialize.

To make matters worse, primary balances are projected to weaken further owing to the demographic shock.

- For the EU-25 countries, Eurostat 2008 projections suggest on average a doubling of the old-age dependency ratio (population older than 65 relative to working-age population) from 2005 to 2050, with the modal age-cohorts moving from mid-thirties to late fifties. These changes will exert upward pressure on public spending for pensions and health care (Table 6.3). The European Commission (EC, 2006) projects that for the EU-25, average spending will increase by 3.4 percent of

Table 6.1. Historical Episodes of Major Accumulations and Decumulations of Government Debt
(As a share of GDP, in percent)

	Accumulation	Cause	Debt Decumulation	Method of Debt/GDP Ratio Reduction
Postwar hyperinflations				
Germany	From 63 in 1913 to 72 in 1919 (excluding war reparations).	World War I.	95 percent of debt value cut by 1923.	Hyperinflation (1921–23), supported by double-digit real growth.
Japan	From 23 in 1919 to 40 by 1929, rising sharply after 1937 to 204 (peak in 1944).	Tokyo earthquake (1923); financial crisis (1927); Japan-China War (1937); World War II.	To 56 in 1946.	Hyperinflation.
Postwar economic growth and expenditure reductions				
United Kingdom	From 90 in 1795 to 160 in 1816, peaking at 185 in 1822.	Napoleonic wars; followed by sharp deflation.	To 30 by 1914, with minor interruptions.	Sharp peacetime decline in military spending; healthy growth; fiscal balance or surplus was the norm.
United States	From 16 in 1929 to 40 over 1933–38; then peaking at 121 in 1946.	Great Depression; World War II.	To 50 by 1965.	Rapid real growth; also, expenditure cuts and some inflation.
Japan	From 23 in 1903 to 71 in 1910.	Japanese-Russian War (and aftermath); associated rise in risk premia on foreign debt.	To 23 by 1919.	Fiscal tightening; mandated contributions to debt consolidation fund; reduced risk premium on foreign debt after victory against Russia; rapid growth.
Decumulation through virtuous circles of fiscal adjustment and rapid growth				
Ireland	From 64 in 1979 to 109 in 1987.	Prolonged macrofiscal problems; large interventionist public sector.	To 38 by 2000; 25 by 2007.	Strong growth and fiscal adjustment; tax base widening stabilized revenues despite lowering of rates; sharp decline in debt interest costs with improved debt management.
Denmark	From 47 in 1980 to 82 in 1984, stabilizing there until 1993.	Growth slowdown; large fiscal deficits.	To 45 in 2000.	Growth pickup, supported by expenditure-led fiscal reforms.
Belgium	From 61 in 1976 to 132 in 1993.	Large primary deficits, growth slowdown, higher interest costs.	To 85 in 2007.	Initially through tax increases, lower interest costs, and revival of growth; lately through balanced budgets and moderate growth.
Canada	From 47 in 1981 to 102 in 1996.	Large structural deficits, cyclical downturn, soaring interest rates in early 1980s.	To 64 in 2007.	Robust growth, sharp and enduring expenditure cuts at federal level matched by similar rationalization at provincial and community levels.
Netherlands	From 40 in 1979 to 79 in 1993.	Growth slowdown; interest rate hike in early 1980s; intermittent rise in structural deficits.	To 51 in 2001.	Sharp expenditure reduction that permitted growth-enhancing tax cuts.
Decumulation through mixes of inflation, declines in risk premia, growth, and fiscal adjustment				
France	From 67 in 1913 to 140 in 1919, rising further to 185 by 1922.	World War I; postwar political deadlock over distribution of fiscal adjustment burden.	To 139 by 1925; 100 by 1929.	Initial decline driven by inflation and growth, followed later by increases in income taxes on middle classes and indirect taxes (1926–29); policy to keep the franc from appreciating also helped; high share of short-term debt prevented recourse to inflating away debt unfront.
United Kingdom	From 26 in 1913 to 130 in 1919, rising gradually to 178 in 1933.	World War I, zero growth in the 1920s; Great Depression (1929–33).	To 141 by 1938.	Debt reduction was slow and limited because, with fiscal balance maintained during 1919–33, growth was weak. Subsequently, abandonment of gold standard allowed the pound to depreciate which, in turn, helped reduced real interest rates and spur growth.

Figure 6.2. Selected Countries: Public Debt-to-GDP Ratio
(In percent)

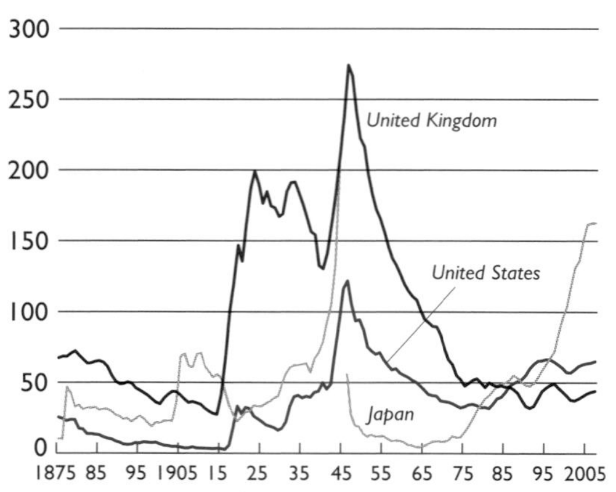

Sources: United Kingdom: Goodhart (1999) and IMF, World Economic Outlook database. United States: *Historical Statistics of the United States*, Millennial Edition Online; Office of Management and Budget; and U.S. Census Bureau. Japan: Bank of Japan, *Hundred-Year Statistics of the Japanese Economy*; and Toyo Keizai Shinposa, *Estimates of Long-Term Economic Statistics of Japan Since 1868*. Data for Japan refer to the central government.

GDP, with an increase in pension expenditures of 2.3 percent of GDP, and the rest accounted for by health and long-term care spending.[26]

- For the United States, the Congressional Budget Office (CBO) projects annual federal budget spending on pensions to increase from 4.3 percent to 6.1 percent of GDP from 2007 to 2050 (CBO, 2007).[27] Significant aging-related budgetary pressures are also present in Japan, particularly from spending on health and long-term care.

- While less affected, the share of the populations older than 65 is projected to increase in all emerging economies, with the old-age dependency ratio expected to triple, on average, by 2050 (United Nations, 2006). Korea faces the steepest increase,

but there are also significant pressures in China and many other countries (Figure 6.3). Outside the G-20 countries, demographic trends are expected to be particularly negative in most of central and eastern Europe. Overall, budgetary aging-related spending is likely to increase in emerging economies, but given the smaller role of the public sector in the provision of pensions and health care (with some exceptions such as in eastern Europe), less so than in advanced economies.

- An illustrative additional "cost pressure" scenario (Table 6.3, 2050 CPS columns) indicates that budget strains could be substantially larger if the increase in the relative price of health and long-term care services are higher than assumed in the relatively conservative baseline scenario. The high income elasticity shown by the price of these services in many countries and the rapid increase in social demand for them make this alternative scenario a plausible possibility.[28]

Altogether, the global fiscal outlook is somber. The debt ratio of G-20 advanced countries is projected to increase by an additional 59 percentage points by 2030 (Figure 6.4).[29] Strains are also likely to appear in emerging economies (as demographic forces will operate also there), though long-term projections in those economies are subject to greater uncertainty, owing to data limitations.

The Way Forward

This somber outlook raises two critical, and related, questions:

- Should the economic outlook deteriorate further, how much room does fiscal policy have to continue its supportive action?

- What should be done to reassure markets that fiscal solvency is not at risk?

The issue of how much further room there is for fiscal support cannot be answered in absolute terms, but should be addressed as a risk management issue. Governments will have to balance two opposite risks:

---

[26]The EC projections of pension and health care costs are currently being updated. The baseline scenario assumes that the increase in life expectancy will lead to some postponement of the need for additional care. The health care projections assume an elasticity of demand higher than unity (1.1) in the short term, gradually declining to unity over the projection period.

[27]The relatively small increase in U.S. health care spending in Table 6.3 reflects the fact that only the demographic effect is considered and not the impact of high income elasticity of demand and/or faster growth of health care costs relative to GDP.

---

[28]The above outlook does not take into account, on the one hand, additional costs that may arise for public finances from climate change (IMF, 2008b), and, on the other hand, some savings associated with demographic change, for example, lower costs for education.

[29]The projection assumes an interest rate growth differential as projected in the April 2009 *World Economic Outlook* until 2014 and converging thereafter to 1 percentage point; and pension and health contributions remaining constant as a ratio to GDP after 2014.

Table 6.2. Debt and Primary Balance
(In percent of GDP)

| | Precrisis WEO Projections[1] | | | | Current WEO Projections | | | | Debt-Stabilizing Primary Balance or Primary Balance Needed to Bring Debt to Benchmark Level (Shaded)[2] |
| | Debt | | Primary balance | | Debt | | Primary balance | | |
	2009	2012	2009	2012	2009	2014	2009	2014	
Advanced countries									
Australia	7.8	6.0	0.9	0.6	11.3	16.6	−2.8	−1.0	0.2
Austria	56.8	51.5	2.2	2.0	69.9	66.0	−0.7	2.5	1.0
Belgium	79.2	71.2	3.7	3.5	98.0	109.8	−0.6	−1.7	4.2
Canada	61.0	51.3	1.2	0.5	75.4	66.2	−2.8	0.0	1.0
Denmark	16.1	6.6	3.5	2.3	25.1	28.9	−1.5	−0.9	0.3
Finland	29.6	26.8	3.2	1.8	40.0	54.6	−2.4	−3.0	0.5
France	63.0	60.5	−0.3	0.8	74.9	89.7	−4.1	−1.8	2.7
Germany	61.1	59.4	2.1	2.0	79.4	91.0	−2.4	1.0	2.8
Greece	75.0	70.1	1.5	1.7	104.3	109.7	0.1	−1.0	4.2
Iceland	28.8	27.4	−1.6	−0.6	128.3	79.7	−7.4	5.0	2.0
Ireland	23.6	23.2	0.5	0.4	63.6	126.0	−12.7	−6.7	5.3
Italy	104.1	102.0	2.5	2.6	115.3	129.4	−0.4	0.8	5.6
Japan	194.2	189.6	−1.8	−0.2	217.2	234.2	−8.6	−4.7	9.6
Korea	36.1	35.9	2.2	1.5	40.0	51.8	−1.7	1.9	1.2
Netherlands	42.4	33.1	2.8	2.9	57.9	59.6	−1.6	0.8	0.6
New Zealand	20.8	20.7	2.3	2.1	23.4	53.9	−2.1	−4.6	0.5
Norway	43.8	43.8	13.0	9.6	67.2	67.2	6.9	11.5	1.1
Portugal	63.6	57.0	1.3	2.1	72.8	85.6	−2.8	0.8	2.4
Spain	32.4	29.7	1.6	1.5	51.8	69.2	−6.3	−1.9	1.2
Sweden	33.6	21.1	2.1	2.7	39.9	39.3	−3.6	0.8	0.4
United Kingdom	42.9	42.5	−0.5	0.2	62.7	87.8	−7.8	−3.1	2.6
United States	63.4	65.8	−0.8	−0.3	87.0	106.7	−12.5	0.4	3.9
Emerging market economies									
Argentina	51.0	39.6	2.8	2.4	50.4	48.5	0.4	0.9	1.0
Brazil	67.7	62.7	3.4	3.4	65.4	54.1	2.8	3.5	1.4
Bulgaria	20.8	15.6	3.1	1.1	19.4	16.4	1.8	0.0	0.2
Chile	3.8	2.8	4.4	3.1	3.3	1.5	−3.0	1.3	0.0
China	13.4	11.2	−0.4	−0.6	19.8	17.9	−3.1	0.3	0.2
Hungary	66.0	65.6	0.3	0.2	75.9	59.0	1.5	4.3	1.7
India	69.8	61.6	0.2	0.5	86.8	76.8	−4.3	0.7	3.0
Indonesia	32.8	27.7	0.1	0.6	32.9	31.0	−0.5	0.3	0.3
Malaysia	40.7	35.8	−1.1	−1.6	38.6	50.1	−3.3	−5.2	1.1
Mexico	40.9	41.3	0.9	0.2	46.9	44.0	−0.9	−0.1	0.7
Nigeria	11.1	8.9	8.1	4.2	9.7	13.0	−7.3	2.2	0.1
Pakistan	48.9	43.2	0.7	0.5	56.9	48.8	0.6	0.6	1.0
Philippines	46.1	42.7	2.2	1.9	50.1	44.2	2.2	2.2	0.7
Poland	45.6	44.6	−0.7	−0.2	50.9	52.1	−1.8	0.6	1.3
Russia	3.9	2.3	1.7	1.5	6.9	9.6	−5.7	−4.0	0.1
Saudi Arabia	14.8	11.4	19.2	16.8	15.6	7.9	−3.3	6.3	0.1
South Africa	24.0	18.1	2.5	1.9	29.1	29.9	−0.7	0.0	0.3
Turkey[3]	48.7	37.3	6.3	6.3	47.2	53.7	−0.2	1.7	1.4
Ukraine	13.5	12.1	−1.7	−1.6	19.3	15.1	−2.8	−1.5	0.1

Sources: IMF, *World Economic Outlook (WEO)*, April 2009; and IMF staff calculations.

[1]IMF, *World Economic Outlook*, October 2007. A direct comparison for Turkey cannot be made, as postcrisis numbers reflect a substantial revision in the GDP series.

[2]Average primary balance needed to stabilize debt at end-2014 level if the respective debt-to-GDP ratio is less than 60 percent for advanced economies or 40 percent for emerging market economies (no shading); or to bring debt ratio to 60 percent (halve for Japan and reduce to 40 percent for emerging market economies) in 2029 (shaded entries). The analysis is illustrative and makes some simplifying assumptions: in particular, beyond 2014, an interest rate–growth rate differential of 1 percent is assumed, regardless of country-specific circumstances; moreover, the projections are "passive" scenarios based on constant policies. The primary balances reported in this table include interest revenue, which could be sizable in some countries.

[3]Fiscal projections reflect IMF staff's estimates based on the authorities' policy intentions as stated in the EU Pre-Accession Program document.

Table 6.3. Fiscal Costs of Aging
(In percent of GDP)

	Pension		Health			Long-Term Health Care			Total Increase[2]
	t	2050	2005	2050	2050 CPS[1]	2005	2050	2050 CPS[1]	
Australia	3.0 (2000)	4.6	5.6	6.5	9.7	0.9	2.2	2.9	3.8
Canada	5.1 (2000)	10.9	6.2	7	10.2	1.2	2.3	3.2	7.7
France	12.8 (2004)	14.8	7	7.3	10.6	1.1	2.3	2.8	3.5
Germany	11.4 (2004)	13.1	7.8	8.2	11.4	1	1.9	2.9	3
Italy	14.2 (2004)	14.7	6	6.5	9.7	0.6	2	3.5	2.4
Japan	7.9 (2000)	8.5	6	7.1	10.3	0.9	2.3	3.1	3.1
Korea	2.1 (2000)	10.1	3	4.6	7.8	0.3	4.1	4.1	13.4
Mexico	...	...	3	4.3	7.5	0.1	2	4.2	3.2
Russia	5.4 (2006)	8.4	3.2	3.3	...	...	...	...	3.2
Spain	8.6 (2004)	15.7	5.5	6.4	9.6	0.2	1	2.6	8.8
Turkey	...	...	5.9	6.7	9.9	0.1	1.8	1.8	2.5
United Kingdom	6.6 (2004)	8.6	6.1	6.5	9.7	1.1	2.1	3	3.4
United States	4.3 (2007)	6.1	6.3	6.5	9.7	0.9	1.8	2.7	2.9

Sources: Organization for Economic Cooperation and Development (2001 and 2006); European Commission (2006); Hauner (2008); World Bank (2006); and Congressional Budget Office (2007). Data for other G-20 countries were not available.

[1]CPS = cost pressure scenario. For health spending, assumes additional 1 percent annual growth in spending on top of the demographic and income effect. For long-term health care, it assumes full "Baumol" effect, that is, long-term costs per dependent increase.

[2]Total increase includes change in the fiscal cost of aging due to pension, health, and long-term health care between t and 2050 for the base-case scenario only.

- *The risk of prolonged depression and stagnation.* From this perspective, the economic and fiscal costs of inaction could be even larger than the costs of action. The higher this risk, the more it will be necessary for governments to take risks on the fiscal side by providing further support (to the financial sector—as a key priority—but possibly also to directly support aggregate demand).[30]

- *The risk of a loss of confidence in government solvency.* Fiscal balances are expected to deteriorate in bad times. But the risks have increased and there is a need to closely monitor developments in real interest rates, spreads, and debt maturity. The more these indicators weaken, the less would be the room for further fiscal action.[31]

Balancing these risks will be challenging but the trade-off can be improved if governments clarify, in a credible way, their strategy to ensure fiscal solvency.

Indeed, greater clarity is urgently needed. The problem cannot simply be ignored.

A strategy to ensure fiscal solvency should be based on four pillars:

- Fiscal stimulus packages should consist as much as possible of temporary measures;

- Policies should be cast within medium-term fiscal frameworks that envisage a gradual fiscal correction, once economic conditions improve, with proper arrangements to monitor progress;

- Governments should pursue growth enhancing structural reforms; and

- There should be a firm commitment and a clear strategy to contain the trend increase in aging-related spending in countries exposed to unsustainable demographic shocks.

These prescriptions are, of course, not new. Some of them are part of the long-standing policy advice provided by the IMF. However, the weaker state of public finances has now raised the cost of inaction.

The Composition of the Stimulus Package

The fiscal stimulus should not raise deficits permanently. As noted in Spilimbergo and others (2008), fiscal stimulus measures will likely have to be prolonged—

---

[30]To the extent that fiscal action is effective in supporting growth, its net fiscal cost is reduced by the automatic stabilizers. For example, the net cost of a 1 percentage point of GDP of fiscal stimulus, assuming a unit multiplier, is about ¾ percentage point of GDP for the G-20. More generally, if fiscal action succeeds in rescuing the economy from a downward expectations spiral, its long-run costs could be lower than in the absence of intervention.

[31]Indeed, as noted in Spilimbergo and others (2008), even in 2008, not all countries were in a position to implement fiscal stimulus.

Figure 6.3. Population Aging in Emerging Market Countries, 2005 and 2050
(Old-age dependency ratio)[1]

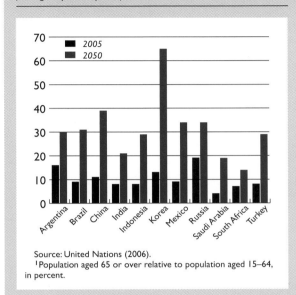

Source: United Nations (2006).
[1]Population aged 65 or over relative to population aged 15–64, in percent.

Figure 6.4. Advanced G-20 Countries: Government Debt[1,2]
(In percent of GDP)

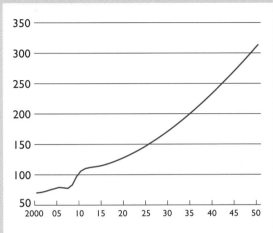

Source: IMF, *World Economic Outlook (WEO)*, April 2009 projections up to 2014.
[1]After 2014, projections assume (1) structural primary balance deteriorates due to demographic factors (Table 6.3); (2) if the debt-to-GDP ratio falls below 20 percent, the fiscal balance loosens to ensure the debt ratio remains above 20 percent; in the case of Korea, which faces particularly severe demographic pressures, the debt ratio is permitted to fall below 20 percent; and (3) the interest rate/growth differential converges to 1 percentage point.
[2]Debt data correspond to general government if available, otherwise most comprehensive fiscal aggregate reported in the *WEO*. Averages based on PPP GDP weights.

because the decline in private sector demand is likely to be long-lasting—but should not be permanent. Ideally, what is needed is an intertemporal shift that, with respect to the precrisis baseline, raises deficits for the expected duration of the crisis and reduces them later, so as to leave long-run debt levels unchanged. Stimulus measures (or sets of measures) should thus be self-reversing, to the extent possible, or at least temporary.

Thus far, not all the stimulus provided conforms to this prescription. The deficit increases related to automatic stabilizers will, of course, be reversed when output recovers, but only part of the announced stimulus packages involves temporary or self-reversing measures. It will, therefore, be important that governments indicate at an early stage how these measures will be offset over the medium term.

Medium-Term Fiscal Frameworks

Ensuring fiscal solvency would be facilitated by medium-term fiscal and debt targets buttressed by a clear adjustment strategy and strong institutional setup (Kumar and Ter-Minassian, 2007). Governments should have a medium-term plan on how to move public finances back to a more sustainable level, backed up by clear policies and supported, where appropriate, by fiscal responsibility laws, fiscal rules, or independent fiscal councils. With the recovery, this approach would help mitigate pres-

sures from procyclical spending increases or tax cuts, allowing more robust buffers to be built. Such an approach has been followed successfully by some countries that had to face a surge of government debt as a result of financial crises (Box 6.2; see also Henriksson, 2007). More specifically:

- Medium-term frameworks setting credible targets over the following four–five years can help clarify vulnerabilities, and impel policymakers to take steps to improve the medium-term viability of public finances. But stating medium-term targets is not sufficient: the credibility of these targets—more than in the past—should be buttressed by the definition of clear policy actions through which they will be reached. This is not always the practice in countries with medium-term scenarios.

- To capture fiscal risks, such frameworks should also assess debt solvency under different scenarios. This is particularly important in the current context in which the contingent liabilities of governments have increased.

Box 6.2. Post-Banking-Crisis Fiscal Consolidation: Finland and Sweden During the 1990s

In the early 1990s, both Finland and Sweden experienced recession and sharply deteriorating fiscal positions following major banking crises. The general government balances of both countries deteriorated by about 14 percent of GDP from 1990 to 1993, to –8 percent of GDP in Finland and –11 percent of GDP in Sweden. This contributed to a substantial increase in general government debt, up to 58 percent of GDP in Finland and 72 percent of GDP in Sweden by the mid-1990s, some of which was attributable to the gross direct fiscal costs of the banking crises, estimated at 13 and 4 percent of GDP for Finland and Sweden, respectively. The fiscal expansions in 1992–94 fueled anxiety over fiscal indiscipline; moreover, they did not stimulate private sector activity, because they preceded the financial sector resolution. Thus, risk premia spiked in 1994.

To restore sustainability, fiscal consolidation programs were adopted, based primarily on spending restraint and supported by institutional reforms.

In Finland, two key reforms were adopted. First, a medium-term expenditure framework was introduced to prioritize resource use in a strategic and transparent manner, and to provide spending departments with greater autonomy in managing their resources. Second, entitlements

were reformed to reduce spending and structurally increase employment. This included tighter qualification rules and temporary lifting of inflation adjustment for unemployment benefits; reduction of benefits for early retirement; and determination of the pensionable wage on the basis of the last 10 (rather than 4) years of employment.

In Sweden, the authorities implemented a Consolidation Program aimed at achieving fiscal balance. Key measures included: tighter rules on transfers to households (housing grants and subsidies, sick leave benefits, unemployment insurance, family allowances and social insurance benefits); and revenue enhancing measures, such as increases in income taxes, social security fees, and employee payroll taxes.

These fiscal consolidations helped entrench the economic recovery (post-1994) and reduce general government debt/GDP ratios to below 45 percent in Finland and 55 percent in Sweden by 2000. The economic recovery, which contributed to the improvement in the fiscal position, was led by falling interest rates and the rise in exports (following the currency devaluations and the restoration of financial sector health). The redirection of policy toward fiscal balance reduced interest rates and reinforced the economic turnaround.

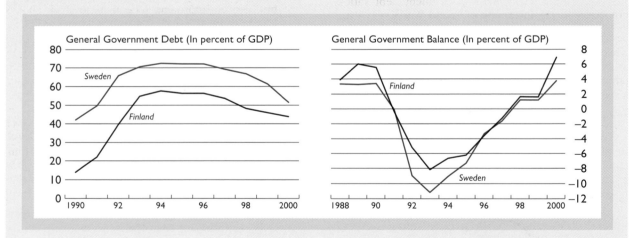

- Effective and transparent processes should be set in place to maximize revenues from management and recovery of assets acquired during the financial support operations. Losses incurred by central banks as a result of support to financial institutions should be promptly covered through transfers recorded in the government's budget.

- Fiscal rules may help to maintain or restore solvency if they are supported by the requisite political commitment, allow sufficient flexibility to

respond to exceptional circumstances, and are designed and implemented in a way that avoids excessive constraints on policy or is simply nonbinding. Whether or not formal rules are introduced, governments should be committed to tighten fiscal policy in good times, now that fiscal policy has been relaxed during bad times.

- A complementary role can be played by fiscal councils, already established in many countries, to provide independent monitoring and forecasts.

Table 6.4. Emerging Economies: Selected Debt Reduction Episodes
(In percent of GDP)

Country/Time Period	Initial Level of Debt	Debt Reduction	Contribution to Debt Reduction			
			Primary surplus	Growth-interest rate differential	Real exchange rate appreciation	Other
Poland (1993–98)	84.3	47.7	3.3	22.6	9.6	12.1
Chile (1990–98)	45.9	33.0	30.0	11.5	3.9	–12.5
Ecuador (1988–90)	113.5	32.1	4.1	11.4	–11.8	28.4
Pakistan (2001–07)	84.8	29.7	6.4	17.1	5.1	1.0
Egypt (2003–07)	114.9	27.7	–11.0	29.9	1.9	6.8
Jamaica (2002–07)	122.0	27.4	50.8	–30.3	3.8	3.2
Brazil (2002–05)	85.0	20.8	12.4	1.7	4.6	2.1
Colombia (2002–07)	49.8	16.4	14.4	1.0	4.6	–3.6
Malaysia (2003–07)	44.4	14.5	–4.3	8.3	2.4	8.1
Tunisia (2001–07)	62.7	11.8	–0.7	8.1	6.4	–2.0
Average (unweighted)	80.7	26.1	10.6	8.1	3.0	4.4

Sources: IMF, *World Economic Outlook*; and IMF staff estimates.

Growth-Enhancing Structural Reforms

Rapid growth has been a key factor in bringing about sustained improvements in government debt ratios. For example, the aftermath of World War I saw a further increase in the debt ratios in several advanced economies (e.g., France and the United Kingdom) as a result of the Great Depression, whereas the aftermath of World War II was characterized by declining debt ratios fostered by rapid economic growth (Table 6.1). Strong growth has also been a key source of debt reduction in more recent emerging market episodes (Table 6.4; see also World Bank, 2005; and IMF, 2005).

Thus, together with other structural reforms, expenditure and tax policies will need to focus on fostering growth (Daniel and others, 2006; Gupta, Clements, and Inchauste, 2004). Expenditure-led adjustments supported by tax base broadening, creating scope for tax rate reductions, have in some cases reduced interest costs and spurred economic growth, resulting in especially successful debt reductions (see Box 6.2). More specifically:

- *Expenditure policies.* The fiscal stimulus measures that are being adopted should be consistent with boosting growth potential. Similarly, in identifying the measures needed to consolidate the fiscal accounts, governments should seek to reduce unproductive spending while preserving expenditures that are likely to yield high-quality growth and a high social rate of return (e.g., basic transportation infrastructure, education, preventive health care). Distributional objectives should be pursued by targeted spending measures.

- *Tax reform.* Reforms should focus not only on broadening the tax base and reducing rates, so as to minimize distortions and promote equity, but also on improving incentives to work and to invest, simplifying administration and compliance, and enhancing the transparency of the tax code. Changes to the tax structure should give greater emphasis—beyond externality-correcting taxes (e.g., carbon pricing schemes)—to consumption taxes (especially a broad-based VAT) and property taxes (with income tax and benefit systems addressing equity considerations more directly) and to reducing remaining taxes on international trade. It will also be important to reduce the bias in favor of debt vis-à-vis equity financing, present in most tax systems.

Containing Age-Related Spending

Two considerations are relevant in the current context:

- In spite of the large fiscal costs of the crisis, the major threat to long-term fiscal solvency is still represented, at least in advanced countries, by unfavorable demographic trends. Net present value calculations illustrate the differential impact of the crisis vis-à-vis aging: in particular, for advanced countries, the fiscal burden of the crisis is about 11 percent of the aging-related costs (Table 6.5, last column). Addressing pressures arising from aging can go a long way in allaying market concerns about fiscal solvency, in spite of the current fiscal weakening.

Table 6.5. Net Present Value of Impact on Fiscal Deficit of Crisis and Aging-Related Spending[1,2]
(In percent of GDP, unless otherwise indicated)

Country	Crisis	Aging	Crisis/Aging
Australia	30	482	6.1
Canada	21	726	2.9
France	31	276	11.2
Germany	29	280	10.3
Italy	35	169	20.7
Japan	35	158	22.3
Korea	20	683	2.9
Mexico	13	261	4.8
Spain	39	652	5.9
Turkey	22	204	10.9
United Kingdom	48	335	14.2
United States	37	495	7.5
Advanced G-20 countries	35	409	10.8

Source: IMF staff estimates.

[1]Table reports net present value of the impact on fiscal balance of the crisis and of aging-related spending. Source data for advanced G-20 economies are OECD (2001) and EC (2006); see also Table 6.3. The third column reports the ratio of the first column to the second column in percent. The discount rate used is 1 percent a year in excess of GDP growth for each country. Given that real growth is expected to average 3 percent a year, this is equivalent to applying an average real discount rate of 4 percent a year. For years after 2050, the calculation assumes the impact is the same as in 2050.

[2]Averages based on PPP GDP weights.

• The strategy followed so far in many advanced countries (notably in Europe) has focused not only on entitlement reforms, but also on prepositioning the fiscal accounts for the demographic shock, by cutting the level of debt and reducing spending in other areas (or keeping relatively high tax rates) to make room for expected future increases in pension and health spending. However, this strategy has been derailed, or at least delayed, by the crisis (see Figure 6.5, reporting the pre- and post-crisis outlook in the fiscal balances of five large European countries).

The fiscal impact of the crisis thus reinforces the urgency of entitlement reform. With larger headline debt and lower primary balances, pressures from aging will need to be addressed directly by reforming pension and health entitlements. The amount and speed of adjustment should be country-specific, depending on factors such as demographic and economic growth prospects, cost of borrowing, debt tolerance, and public attitudes toward the tax burden, expenditure needs, and the size of the public sector. Nevertheless, for most countries, postponing required reforms would likely result in larger and more painful adjustment in later years. Moreover, compared with the previously pursued strategy of prepositioning the fiscal accounts for the demographic shock, a direct reform of health and pension entitlements may have some advantages, as it involves smaller cuts in other priority spending (or lower taxation).

Effective entitlement reform should abide by well-known principles. In the area of pensions, savings must be attained while sufficiently preserving intergenera-

Figure 6.5. EU-5 Countries: Outlook for Fiscal Balance Versus 2006 Stability Program[1]
(In percent of GDP)

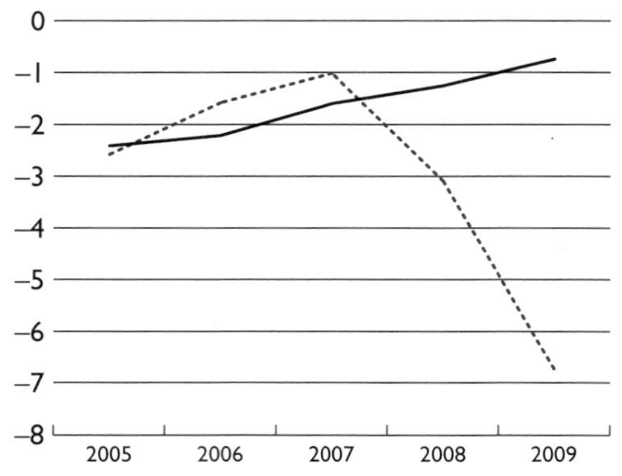

Sources:
[1]Solid line refers to 2006 Stability Program. Dashed line refers to IMF, *World Economic Outlook (WEO)*, April 2009 estimates and projections. EU-5 denotes simple average of France, Germany, Italy, Spain, and the United Kingdom.

tional equity. The main tool should be increases in the effective retirement age, although other parametric changes may be needed. Any assistance to funded pension plans that incurred major losses as a result of the financial crisis should be targeted to lower-income households for whom current retirement income is likely to be seriously reduced. Regarding health care, reforms will need to be equitable to secure broad public support when limiting the service coverage, or shifting costs to the private sector (Verhoeven, Gunnarsson, and Carcillo, 2007).

A specific challenge in the current conjuncture is to take early action in these areas without undermining ongoing efforts to jumpstart economic growth. The key objective should be to ensure that entitlement reform yields savings for the government without reducing aggregate demand. Some steps are less controversial, from an economic perspective. For example, in the area of pensions, an increase in the retirement age would seem unlikely to lead to a decline in consumption. Other steps are more controversial: an increase in contribution rates would reduce workers' disposable incomes and, as a result, consumption; this latter type of measure would thus seem less desirable in the current conjuncture. In the area of health care, while most countries will need to limit the types of services covered under public systems to ensure solvency, reforms aimed at expanding the provision of basic health care coverage to greater shares of the population—in countries where no major fiscal correction is needed even after the crisis—could help reduce precautionary savings by households. Consideration could also be given to reducing entitlements in a gradual way so that any adverse economic reaction would be spread out over time. What is critical, in any case, is the clear communication of a stronger commitment than in the past to address entitlement reforms decisively, supported by the identification of the necessary actions and their timing.

Enacting major reforms in this area at times of severe economic weakening is likely to be challenging from a political economy perspective, but there are opportunities too. If the fiscal stimulus succeeds in supporting activity, the climate for reform would also improve. Indeed, it may also be that the crisis environment offers in some countries an opportunity for a comprehensive "big bang" approach, where a strong package of immediate stimulus to support the economy would provide the quid pro quo for the introduction of long-lasting reforms in entitlements and other areas. Moreover, times of crisis have in the past provided opportunities for enacting politically difficult reforms.

Appendix I   Reporting the Fiscal Impact of Financial Sector Support

A thorough and transparent reporting of government interventions in the financial sector is a prerequisite for understanding the fiscal stance in crisis countries and prescribing appropriate fiscal policy. This appendix discusses how to report the fiscal impact of various forms of government intervention.[32] The first section deals with the reporting of direct government interventions in bank restructuring operations. To do so, it presents a number of principles for reporting public intervention in resolving financial crises, drawing on accepted statistical methodologies such as the IMF's *Government Finance Statistics Manual* (*GFSM 1986* and *GFSM 2001*)—the usual basis for IMF staff monitoring of the fiscal position.[33] The second section describes the reporting of indirect interventions, notably those giving rise to contingent liabilities.

Reporting the Cost of Direct Interventions

When government intervenes in a financial institution, the key question for reporting purposes is whether the intervention creates an effective government claim on the institution.[34] The nature (or quality) of the claim determines the statistical treatment.

- If the government's intervention results in an increase in its claims on financial institutions commensurate to its intervention and for which the government expects to get returns (equity purchases) or be repaid (loans to a solvent bank), the intervention would be recorded as a financing operation, since it does not change the government's net worth. It simply changes the composition of its assets and/or liabilities.

- An unrequited intervention should, however, be treated as an expense (capital or current transfer) as it results directly in a reduction in the government's net worth. An important example is the case of the recapitalization of a bank by government that does not create new claims for the government (meaning that the recapitalization is an unrequited transfer) nor a positive expectation of recovering associated claims (e.g., when assets exist but are impaired).

Under cash accounting (e.g., *GFSM 1986* or the cash statement in *GFSM 2001*), the fiscal impact of some government noncash interventions is not fully reflected in the fiscal balance. Only the carrying cost of these interventions would be reported above the line (as interest payments) and increase the fiscal deficit. To remedy this shortcoming, Daniel, Davis, and Wolfe (1997) proposed an "augmented" fiscal balance as a means of capturing the full costs of recapitalization: as is the case with cash operations, noncash bank assistance operations (e.g., recapitalization through transfer of public debt, and debt swap) would count toward the "augmented" deficit and add to government debt if implemented for purposes of public policy. Table A1.1 and Table A1.2 present the treatment of similar operations under *GFSM 1986* and *GFSM 2001*, respectively, using numerical examples.

The *GFSM 2001* provides a more complete framework for reporting direct government restructuring operations, focusing on the government's net worth and integrating stocks and flows as well as cash transactions.[35]

- *Flow operations* are reflected in fiscal indicators such as the operating balance, net lending/borrowing balance, and the cash surplus/deficit. In addition, *GFSM 2001* allows (¶4.45) a classification of financial assets according to whether they have been acquired/disposed of for public policy or liquidity management purposes, as transactions in policy-related assets often involve a subsidy component. While this classification is usually not included in the reported *GFSM 2001* data, policy-related

---

[32]This appendix does not address issues related to accounting principles.

[33]Both government finance statistics manuals are available via the Internet at http://www.imf.org/external/pubs/ft/gfs/manual/gfs.htm.

[34]This criterion was not developed at the time of *GFSM 1986*. All transactions in claims on others acquired for purposes of public policy would be captured by "lending minus repayments" above-the-line. If the government intervention does not result in an effective claim, it would be recorded as expenditure.

[35]The treatment of direct interventions is essentially the same under the EU European System of Accounts 1995 (ESA-95).

changes in net assets can be treated as flows with characteristics similar to revenue and expense for analytical purposes. Such treatment is notably used in compiling the overall fiscal balance,[36] similar to the "augmented" fiscal balance proposed by Daniel, Davis, and Wolfe (1997) under *GFSM 1986*.

- *Stock information*, such as the government's balance sheet, permits a better understanding of changes in the government's net worth. The values of assets and liabilities at the beginning of the reporting period plus the transactions recorded in the standard government operations table ("statement of government operations") and the "statement of other economic flows" determine their values at the end of the period. "Other economic flows" comprise valuation changes and a variety of other economic events, such as debt write-offs, that affect the holdings of assets and liabilities (see below). Their proper reporting is essential for understanding the impact on government of changes in the value of assets and liabilities, and thereby of the government's net worth.

The main types of direct intervention should be recorded on the basis of the following principles (references to the columns below correspond to the proposed treatment of the discussed operation in Table A1.1 (*GFSM 1986*) or Table A1.2 (*GFSM 2001*)):

- *Loans to financial institutions and investments in equity of financial institutions* (requited recapitalization) are recorded as the acquisition of a financial asset (columns i–ii): In the case of loans extended, subsequent interest/dividends and amortization repaid by the financial institution are recorded as government revenue and a reduction in financial assets, respectively. The transactions themselves (extension of a loan, investment in equity, and so on) are therefore not reflected in net lending/borrowing, as they do not affect the government's net worth as long as the value of the loan or investment remains unimpaired.[37] However, as the government's new asset was acquired for public policy purposes, it would be reflected in the overall fiscal balance. Conversely, if the loan or investment in equity does not raise an effective asset (i.e., the intervened institution is "worthless") then the treatment becomes similar to the "unrequited recapitalization" below (i.e., it reduces the government's net worth).

- *Unrequited recapitalization* (i.e., not involving an exchange of assets) through a capital injection (column iii) or the assumption of a failed bank's liabilities (columns iv–v) is recorded, along with the corresponding carrying costs, as an expense in the operating statement. The full costs of bank recapitalization are thus reflected in net lending/borrowing.

- *The purchase of troubled assets* will be recorded simply as the acquisition of a financial asset when it is settled at market/fair value (column vi). It will, therefore, affect the overall fiscal balance (as the purchase is made for public policy purposes), but not net lending/borrowing.[38] The purchase will, however, require the recording of an expense when it is settled above market/fair value (the expense will then amount to the premium paid by the government relative to market/fair value, column vii).

A few further issues to keep in mind when recording government interventions:

- *Critical to the proper reporting of a government intervention is its valuation.* In some operations, such as the purchase of troubled assets, the current market value of some of the assets may be difficult to determine. The valuation of these assets is, however, crucial in defining the exact nature of the government intervention, i.e., whether it involves a degree of active fiscal policy, or is solely for liquidity management purposes. For example, in the case of the purchase by a government of troubled assets from financial companies, the price that the government will pay will determine whether this operation is purely an asset swap, providing the financial institutions with more liquid assets (cash or government securities vs. troubled assets), or whether it also aims at recapitalizing these institutions (by valuing these assets higher than their estimated market price/fair value). *GFSM 2001* stipulates that (¶9.12): "If the market value can be determined, then the transaction should be valued at that amount and a second transaction should be recorded as an expense to account for the transfer. Otherwise, the value of the transaction should be the amount of funds exchanged." However, when there is a strong presumption that the assets are severely impaired and bought at a significant premium, there may be a strong rationale for reporting the estimated implicit subsidy as an expense.

- In the absence of an *observable market price* for these assets/liabilities, other rules need to be set

---

[36]The overall fiscal balance is defined (*GFSM 2001*, Box 4.1) as "net lending/borrowing adjusted through the rearrangement of lending and repayment transactions in assets and liabilities that are deemed to be for public policy purposes."

[37]The net impact of this intervention would be interest receivable forgone because governments usually extend these loans at rates lower than market rates.

[38]In the case of revenue-generating assets (e.g., loans or mortgage-backed securities), the corresponding revenue will, however, be reported and affect net lending/borrowing.

up, for example, historic returns. An assessment of the fair value of the transaction could be made by using the discounted value of expected future flows, using the value of the counterpart of the transaction (such as the mortgaged property values), or using the price at which similar type of assets trade.

- *Other economic flows.* When assets have been purchased and liabilities incurred, changes in their value should be recorded as other economic flows. Realized or not, gains and losses resulting from changes in the prices of the government's assets and liabilities should be recorded as holding gains/losses. These holding gains and losses are not reported in the statement of government operations, and therefore do not impact the government's net lending/borrowing balance. They are reported in the statement of other economic flows and impact on the government's net financial worth (*GFSM 2001*, Figure 4.1). If a government purchases assets at market value (or fair value if there is no market for these assets at the time of the purchase) and the value of these assets subsequently fall, these losses will at no point impact the net lending/borrowing balance of the government, even once they are realized (i.e., the assets are sold and/or the liabilities are reimbursed). Conversely, if a government purchases assets at above market value/fair value, the premium paid by the government will be reported as an expense at the time of the purchase. This reinforces the point that the valuation of government interventions is crucial to their proper reporting. It also encourages reporting not to be limited to reporting economic flows but also aimed at integrating these flows with corresponding stocks to explain and disclose the government's net worth.

In practice, governments have tried to design their support so it does not affect their deficits—that is, they have maintained claims on financial institutions in almost all cases. Appendix II shows how these operations have been treated in a number of countries. IMF staff faces unavoidable judgment calls in deciding whether the claims have the full value attributed to them by government.

Reporting the Cost of Indirect Interventions

Indirect interventions can potentially have an important fiscal cost and therefore need to be fully reported and, when possible, quantified. These interventions can take the form of operations undertaken by nongovernment entities, notably the central bank, or by the government but without immediate costs, such as blanket guarantees.

Quasifiscal Operations

Some public interventions may be implemented by public entities that are not part of the central or general government. The most common example is central-bank-led restructuring operations. If the central bank does not expect to recover the full value of its support, the government indirectly bears the cost through lower profit transfers and possibly compensating the central bank for its losses. These quasifiscal operations would not be directly reflected on the government operations tables. The IMF's *Manual on Fiscal Transparency* states that "it is important to identify, quantify (where possible), and report on quasi-fiscal activities," and recommends that a statement on quasifiscal activities be included in the budget documentation, together with policy purpose statements and information on the duration and intended beneficiaries of the activity. In countries where such operations have been important, the IMF has used a fiscal presentation that consolidates the government operations with central bank quasifiscal operations. When this is not practical, the central bank/public bank support to the financial sector should at least be shown separately in a memorandum item.

In practice, it will be important to

- *Determine whether separate entities are involved in the restructuring*, and whether these entities are nonmarket producers and should be regarded part of government and be consolidated with the fiscal tables. Governments often create special restructuring agencies or accounts, and these should be included in the relevant sector (e.g., central government, general government).

- *Determine whether an operation implemented by a nongovernmental organization is a quasifiscal activity*, which could, in principle, be duplicated by budgetary measures in the form of an explicit tax, subsidy, or direct expenditure (e.g., a central bank could lend to a bank at below-market conditions).

- *When practical, consolidate quasifiscal operations with the government's fiscal operations, especially when they have significant financial magnitude or create major distortions in fiscal analysis.* Considering that quasifiscal operations are in time likely to affect the government position (through lower revenue/dividends or recapitalization needs), there may be a rationale for reflecting the costs of these operations directly in the government's accounts.

- *When estimating the exact cost of quasifiscal activities proves impractical and contentious, a pragmatic approach is often devised.* For example, one could estimate the cost of any quasifiscal operation that has significant financial magnitude or is deemed to create a major distortion.

Table A1.1 Statistical Treatment of Government Intervention (Under GFSM 1986)

	Baseline: No Intervention	Capital Injection					
		Creating an effective claim				No effective claim (iii)	
		Buy equity (i)		Extend a loan (ii)			
		Payment in cash (i)a	Payment in securities (i)b Augmented treatment	Payment in cash (ii)a	Payment in securities (ii)b Augmented treatment	Payment in cash (iii)a	Payment in securities (iii)b Augmented treatment
(1) Total revenue and grants	150	153	153	152	152	150	150
Of which interest received	0	0	0	2	2	0	0
Of which dividends received	0	3	3	0	0	0	0
(2) = (3) + (4) Total expenditure and lending minus repayments	150	250	155	250	155	250	155
(3) Expenditure	150	150	155	150	155	250	155
Of which interest	0	0	5	0	5	0	5
Of which capital transfers	0	0	0	0	0	100	0
(4) Lending minus repayments	0	100	0	100	0	0	0
Loans	0	0	0	100	0	0	0
Shares and other equity	0	100	0	0	0	0	0
(5) = (1) − (2) Overall balance	0	−97	−2	−98	−3	−100	−5
(6) Noncash bank restructuring measures	0	0	100	0	100	0	100
Loans	0	0	0	0	100	0	0
Shares and other equity	0	0	100	0	0	0	0
Capital transfer	0	0	0	0	0	0	100
(7) = (5) − (6) Augmented balance	0	−97	−102	−98	−103	−100	−105
(7) Total financing	0	97	102	98	103	100	105
Domestic financing	0	97	102	98	103	100	105
Net change in banking deposits (− increase)	0	97	2	98	3	100	5
Issuance of treasury bills	0	0	100	0	100	0	100

Note: Assume amount of the capital injection: 100; interest on government securities issued: 5 percent; interest earned on assets acquired by government: 2 percent; interest on cash deposits of government 0 percent; and dividends on shares and other equity: 3 percent.

Government acquires an effective claim on recipient of financial assistance

(i)a Government injects capital in a financial institution by taking up equity to the value of 100, financed from existing cash resources.

This exchange of cash assets for an asset acquired for policy purposes directly reduces the overall balance. The secondary impact of acquiring the equity generates some dividend, thus increasing the overall balance to the extent that it is more than interest forgone on the cash deposits. Government's gross, as well as net, debt remains unchanged.

(i)b Government injects capital in a financial institution by taking up equity to the value of 100, financed by the issuance of securities.

In the standard GFSM 1986 the acquisition of a financial asset for policy purposes, funded by the incurrence of a liability, has no influence on the overall balance in the absence of cash flows. The secondary impact of the actual interest payable on the securities reduces the overall balance, in so far as it does not match the receivable dividend income. Government's stock of gross debt increases with value of securities issued, but net debt remains unchanged.

(ii)a Government injects capital in a financial institution by extending a loan to the bank, financed from existing cash resources.

This exchange of cash assets for a loan acquired for policy purposes directly reduces the overall balance. The secondary impact of the loan extended is interest receivable, thus increasing the overall balance of government to the extent that it is more than interest forgone on the cash deposit. Government's gross, as well as net, debt remains unchanged.

(ii)b Government injects capital in a financial institution by extending a loan to the bank, financed by the issuance of securities.

In the standard GFSM 1986 the acquisition of a financial asset for policy purposes, funded by the incurrence of a liability, has no influence on the overall balance in the absence of cash flows. The secondary impact of the loan extended is interest receivable, thus increasing the overall balance of government to the extent that it is more than interest payable. Government's gross debt increases with value of securities issued, but net debt remains unchanged.

Government does not acquire an effective claim on recipient of financial assistance

(iii)a Government injects capital in a financial institution but does not acquire an effective claim on the recipient. The injection is financed from existing cash resources.

This capital injection directly reduces the overall balance of government due to the capital transfer. In addition, the overall balance could also decrease to the extent that revenue reduces due to interest forgone on the cash deposits. Government's gross debt remains unchanged, but net debt increases.

(iii)b Government injects capital in a financial institution but does not acquire an effective claim on the recipient. The injection is financed by the issuance of securities.

In the standard GFSM 1986 the capital injection has no influence on the overall balance in the absence of cash flows. The secondary impact of the interest cost payable on the securities reduces the overall balance. Government's gross, as well as net, debt increases with the value of securities issued.

Table A1.1 (concluded)

| | Baseline: No Intervention | Reducing Liabilities of Financial Institutions | | Purchasing Bad Assets from Financial Institutions | | | |
| | | | | At market prices (vi) | | At above-market rates (vii) | |
		Full assumption of debt (iv) Augmented treatment	Assistance with debt reduction (v)	Payment in cash (vi)a	Payment in securities (vi)b Augmented treatment	Payment in cash (vii)a	Payment in securities (vii)b Augmented treatment
(1) Total revenue and grants	150	150	150	152	152	152	152
Of which interest received	0	0	0	2	2	2	2
(2) = (3) + (4) Total expenditure and lending minus repayments	150	155	170	250	155	270	155
(3) Expenditure	150	155	170	150	155	170	155
Of which interest	0	5	0	0	5	0	5
Of which capital transfers	0	0	20	0	0	20	0
(4) Lending minus repayments	0	0	0	100	0	100	0
Loans	0	0	0	100	0	100	0
(5) = (1) – (2) Overall balance	0	–5	–20	–98	–3	–118	–3
(6) Noncash bank restructuring measures	0	100	0	0	100	0	120
Loans	0	0	0	0	100	0	100
Capital transfer	0	100	0	0	0	0	20
(7) = (5) – (6) Augmented balance	0	–105	–20	–98	–103	–118	–123
(7) Total financing	0	105	20	98	103	118	123
Domestic financing	0	105	20	98	103	118	123
Net change in banking deposits (–increase)	0	5	20	98	3	118	3
Issuance of treasury bills	0	0	0	0	0	0	0
Increase in other domestic liabilities	0	100	0	0	100	0	120

Note: Assume interest on government securities issued: 5 percent; interest earned on assets acquired by government: 2 percent; and interest on cash deposits of government 0 percent.

Government assists financial institutions in reducing their liabilities

(iv) Government assumes a bank's liabilities in respect of a loan outstanding, to the value of 100.

(v) Government provides assistance to banks in providing them with some cash to be used in reducing outstanding liabilities to the value of 20.

Government purchases bad assets from financial institutions

(vi)a Government purchases bad assets from a bank at market values of 100, financed from existing cash resources.

(vi)b Government purchases bad assets from a bank at market values of 100, financed by the issuance of securities.

(vii)a Government purchases bad assets from a bank at a price of 120 while market value of the asset is 100—financed from existing cash resources.

(vii)b Government purchases bad assets from a bank at a price of 120 while market value of the asset is 100, financed by the issuance of securities.

In the standard GFSM 1986 the loan assumption has no influence on the overall balance in the absence of cash flows. The secondary impact is a reduction in the overall balance due to the interest payable on the assumed loan. Government's stock of gross, and net, debt increases with value of assumed loan.

This assistance directly reduces the overall balance of government due to the capital transfer. The secondary impact of this assistance is a reduction in the overall balance of government to the extent that revenue reduces due to interest forgone on the cash deposits. Government's stock of gross debt remains unchanged, but net debt increases.

This exchange of cash assets for an asset related to policy purposes directly reduces the overall balance of government. The secondary impact of interest receivable increases the overall balance of government to the extent that it is more than interest forgone on the cash deposit. Government's stock of gross, and net, debt remains unchanged.

In the standard GFSM 1986 the acquisition of a financial asset in exchange of a liability has no influence on the overall balance in the absence of cash flows. The secondary impact of the actual interest cost reduces overall balance, in so far as it does not match the interest income. Government's stock of gross debt increases with value of securities issued, but net debt remains unchanged.

This exchange of cash assets for an asset related to policy purposes directly reduces the overall balance of government. The secondary impact of the asset acquired is interest receivable, thus increasing the overall balance of government to the extent that it is more than interest forgone on the cash deposit. Government's stock of gross debt remains unchanged but net debt increases with 20.

In the standard GFSM 1986 the acquisition of an asset related to policy purposes in exchange for a liability has no influence on the overall balance of government in the absence of cash flows. The secondary impact of the actual interest cost reduces the overall balance, in so far as it does not match the interest income. Government's stock of gross debt increases with the value of securities issued (120), and the net debt increases with 20.

	Baseline: No Intervention	Issuing guarantees (viii)	Assuming One-Off Debt Service of Guaranteed Debt (ix)		Servicing Debt When Guarantee Is Called (x)	
			With creating an effective claim on defaulter (ix)a — Augmented treatment	Without creating an effective claim on defaulter (ix)b — Augmented treatment	With creating an effective claim on defaulter (x)a	Without creating an effective claim on defaulter (x)b
(1) Total revenue and grants	150	150	150	150	152	150
Of which interest received	0	0	0	0	2	0
(2) = (3) + (4) Total expenditure and lending minus repayments	150	150	150	150	250	255
(3) Expenditure	150	150	150	150	150	255
Of which interest	0	0	0	0	0	5
Of which capital transfers	0	0	0	0	0	100
(4) Lending minus repayments	0	0	0	0	100	0
Loans	0	0	0	0	100	0
(5) = (1) – (2) Overall balance	0	0	0	0	–98	–105
(6) Noncash bank restructuring measures	0	0	11	11	0	0
Loans			11	0	0	0
Capital transfer			0	11	0	0
(7) = (5) – (6) Augmented balance	0	0	–11	–11	–98	–105
(7) Total financing	0	0	11	11	98	105
Domestic financing	0	0	11	11	98	105
Net change in banking deposits (–increase)	0	0	0	0	98	105
Increase in other domestic liabilities	0	0	11	11	0	0
Memorandum item: Outstanding guarantees	0	1,000	990	990	900	900

Note: Assume interest on government securities issued: 5 percent; interest earned on assets acquired by government: 2 percent; and interest on cash deposits of government 0 percent.

Government assistance through guarantees

(viii) Government provides support to the industry by issuing guarantees to the total amount of 1,000.

This issuance of guarantees does not affect the overall balance of government because the transaction is not recorded in the operation of government. Government's stock of gross, and net, debt remains unchanged because such guarantees are not regarded as government liabilities until such time as these are called. However, for transparency purposes, record the total outstanding amount of guarantees as a memorandum item on the government accounts.

(ix)a Government assumes the obligation to service a one-off principal (10) and interest (1) payment that was guaranteed due to temporary liquidity constraint of a bank (with creating an effective claim on defaulter).

In the GFSM 1986 the assumption of debt service has no influence on the overall balance of government in the absence of cash flows. Since the bank remains a going concern, government acquires an effective claim on the bank. The secondary impact of interest receivable increases the overall balance of government to the extent that it is more than interest forgone on the cash deposit. Government's stock of gross debt increases and net debt remains unchanged.

(ix)b Government assumes the obligation to service a principal (10) and interest payment (1) that was guaranteed, but due to fundamental insolvency issues, government does not obtain an effective claim on the defaulter bank (without creating an effective claim on defaulter).

In the GFSM 1986 the assumption of the servicing of a guaranteed loan has no influence on the overall balance of government in the absence of cash flows. The overall balance could decrease to the extent that revenue reduces due to interest forgone on the cash deposits. Government's stock of gross debt and net debt increase by 11.

(x)a A guarantee to the value of 100 is called. The defaulting bank is being restructured and government obtains an effective claim on the bank.

This exchange of cash assets for an asset related to policy purposes directly reduces the overall balance of government. Since the bank remains a going concern, government acquires an effective claim on the bank. The secondary impact of interest receivable increases the overall balance to the extent that it is more than interest forgone on the cash deposit. Government's stock of gross, and net, debt remains unchanged, while the stock of outstanding guarantees reduces with the amount of the called guarantee.

(x)b A guarantee to the value of 100 is called. The defaulting bank is insolvent and government does not obtain an effective claim on the bank.

A called guarantee has the same impact as loan assumption, assuming the loan directly reduces the overall balance of government due to the capital transfer. The secondary impact is a further reduction in the overall balance due to the interest payable on the assumed loan. Government's stock of gross, and net, debt increases with value of assumed loan, while outstanding guarantees reduce with the same amount.

Table A1.2. Statistical Treatment of Government Intervention (Under GFSM 2001)

	Baseline: No Intervention	Capital Injection					
		Creating an effective claim				No effective claim (iii)	
		Buy equity (i)		Extend a loan (ii)			
		Payment in cash (i)a	Payment in securities (i)b	Payment in cash (ii)a	Payment in securities (ii)b	Payment in cash (iii)a	Payment in securities (iii)b
(1) Revenue	150	153	153	152	152	150	150
Of which interest received	0	0	0	2	2	0	0
Of which dividends received	0	3	3	0	0	0	0
(2) Expense	100	100	105	100	105	200	205
Of which interest	0	0	5	0	5	0	5
Of which capital transfers	0	0	0	0	0	100	100
(3) = (1) – (2) Net/gross operating balance	50	53	48	52	47	–50	–55
(4) Net acquisition of nonfinancial assets	50	50	50	50	50	50	50
(5) = (3) – (4) Net lending/borrowing	0	3	–2	2	–3	–100	–105
(6) = (7) – (8) Transactions in financial assets and liabilities (financing)	0	3	–2	2	–3	–100	–105
(7) Net acquisition of financial assets	0	3	98	2	97	–100	–5
Of which							
Currency and deposits	0	–97	–2	–98	–3	–100	–5
(7.1) Loans for policy purposes	0	0	0	100	100	0	0
(7.2) Shares and other equity for policy purposes	0	100	100	0	0	0	0
(8) Net incurrence of liabilities	0	0	100	0	100	0	100
Of which							
Securities other than shares	0	0	100	0	100	0	100
Loans	0	0	0	0	0	0	0
(9) = (5) = (7.1) – (7.2) Overall balance	0	–97	–102	–98	–103	–100	–105

Note: Assume amount of the capital injection: 100 percent; interest on government securities issued: 5 percent; interest earned on assets acquired by government: 2 percent; interest on cash deposits of government: 0 percent; and dividends on shares and other equity: 3 percent.

Government acquires an effective claim on recipient of financial assistance

(i)a Government injects capital in a financial institution by taking up equity to the value of 100, financed from existing cash resources.

This exchange of one type of asset for another has no primary impact on net worth of government. The secondary impact of acquiring the equity generates some dividend, thus increasing net worth of government to the extent that it is more than interest forgone on the cash deposits. The implied "cost" of the rescue operation is potential losses in the value of the equity investment. Government's gross, as well as net, debt remains unchanged.

(i)b Government injects capital in a financial institution by taking up equity to the value of 100, financed by the issuance of securities.

This acquisition of a financial asset funded by the incurrence of a liability has no primary impact on the net worth of government. The secondary impact of the actual interest payable on the securities reduces net worth, in so far as it does not match the receivable dividend income. The implied "cost" of the rescue operation is potential losses in the value of the equity investment. Government's stock of gross debt increases with value of securities issued, but net debt remains unchanged.

(ii)a Government injects capital in a financial institution by extending a loan to the bank, financed from existing cash resources.

This exchange of one type of asset for another has no primary impact on net worth of government. The secondary impact of the loan extended is interest receivable, thus increasing net worth of government to the extent that it is more than interest forgone on the cash deposit. The implied "cost" of the rescue operation is potential losses on the loans extended. Government's gross, as well as net, debt remains unchanged.

(ii)b Government injects capital in a financial institution by extending a loan to the bank, financed by the issuance of securities.

This acquisition of a financial asset in exchange for a liability has no primary impact on net worth of government. The secondary impact of the loan extended is interest receivable, thus increasing net worth of government to the extent that it is more than interest payable. The implied "cost" of the rescue operation is potential losses on the loans extended. Government's gross debt increases with value of securities issued, but net debt remains unchanged.

Government does not acquire an effective claim on recipient of financial assistance

(iii)a Government injects capital in a financial institution but does not acquire an effective claim on the recipient. The injection is financed from existing cash resources.

This capital injection directly reduces net worth of government due to the capital transfer. In addition, net worth could also decrease to the extent that revenue reduces due to interest forgone on the cash deposits. The implied "cost" of the rescue operation is the amount provided. Government's gross debt remains unchanged, but net debt increases.

(iii)b Government injects capital in a financial institution but does not acquire an effective claim on the recipient. The injection is financed by the issuance of securities.

This capital injection directly reduces net worth of government due to the capital transfer. In addition, net worth is further reduced by the interest cost payable on the securities. The implied "cost" of the rescue operation is the value of the securities provided. Government's gross, and net, debt increases with the value of the securities issued.

| | Baseline: No Intervention | Reducing Liabilities of Financial Institutions | | Purchasing Bad Assets from Financial Institutions | | | |
| | | Full assumption of debt (iv) | Partial assistance with reduction (v) | At market prices (vi) | | At above-market rates (vii) | |
				Payment in cash (vi)a	Payment in securities (vi)b	Payment in cash (vii)a	Payment in securities (vii)b
(1) Revenue	150	150	150	152	152	152	152
Of which interest received	0	0	0	2	2	2	2
(2) Expense	100	205	120	100	105	120	125
Of which interest	0	5	0	0	5	0	5
Of which capital transfers	0	100	20	0	0	20	20
(3) = (1) – (2) Net/gross operating balance	50	–55	30	52	47	32	27
(4) Net acquisition of nonfinancial assets	50	50	50	50	50	50	50
(5) = (3) – (4) also = (6) Net lending/borrowing	0	–105	–20	2	–3	–18	–23
(6) = (7) – (8) Transactions in financial assets and liabilities (financing)	0	–105	–20	2	–3	–18	–23
(7) Net acquisition of financial assets	0	–5	–20	2	97	–18	97
Of which Currency and deposits	0	–5	–20	–98	–3	–118	–18
(7.1) Loans for policy purposes	0	0	0	100	100	100	100
(8) Net incurrence of liabilities	0	100	0	0	100	0	120
Of which Securities other than shares	0	0	0	0	100	0	120
Loans	0	100	0	0	0	0	0
(9) = (5) – (7.1) Overall balance	0	–105	–20	–98	–103	–118	–123

Note: Assume interest on government securities issued: 5 percent; interest earned on assets acquired by government: 2 percent; and interest on cash deposits of government: 0 percent.

Government assists financial institutions in reducing their liabilities

(iv) Government assumes a bank's liabilities in respect of a loan outstanding, to the value of 100.

This loan assumption directly reduces net worth of government due to the capital transfer. The secondary impact is a further reduction in net worth due to the interest payable on the assumed loan. Government's stock of gross, and net, debt increases with value of assumed loan.

(v) Government provides assistance to the bank in providing it with some cash to be used in reducing outstanding liabilities to the value of 20.

This assistance directly reduces net worth of government due to the capital transfer. The secondary impact of this assistance is a reduction in net worth of government to the extent that revenue reduces due to interest forgone on the cash deposits. Government stock of gross debt remains unchanged, but net debt increases.

Governments purchases bad assets from financial institutions

(vi)a Government purchases bad assets from a bank at market value of 100, financed from existing cash resources.

This exchange of one type of asset for another has no primary impact on net worth of government. The secondary impact of interest receivable increases net worth of government to the extent that it is more than interest forgone on the cash deposit. The implied "cost" of the rescue operation is potential losses on the assets acquired. Government's stock of gross, and net, debt remains unchanged.

(vi)b Government purchases bad assets from a bank at market values of 100, financed by the issuance of securities.

This acquisition of a financial asset in exchange for a liability has no primary impact on the net worth of government. The secondary impact of the actual interest cost reduces net worth, in so far as it does not match the interest income. The implied "cost" of the rescue operation is potential losses on the assets acquired. Government's stock of gross debt increases with value of securities issued, but net debt remains unchanged.

(vii)a Government purchases bad assets from a bank at a price of 120 while market value of the asset is 100, financed from existing cash resources.

This exchange of one type of asset for another (acquired at a cost higher than market value) directly reduces net worth of government by the amount of the difference between the market value and purchasing price. The secondary impact of the asset acquired is interest receivable, thus increasing net worth of government to the extent that it is more than interest forgone on the cash deposit. The implied "cost" of the rescue operation is potential losses on the assets acquired. Government's stock of gross debt remains unchanged but net debt increases by 20.

(vii)b Government purchases bad assets from a bank at a price of 120 while market value of the asset is 100, financed by the issuance of securities.

This acquisition of an asset (at a cost higher than market value) in exchange for a liability directly reduces net worth of government by the amount of the difference between the market value of the asset acquired and the value of the liability issued. The secondary impact of the actual interest cost reduces net worth, in so far as it does not match the interest income. The implied "cost" of the rescue operation is potential losses on the assets acquired. Government's stock of gross debt increases with the value of securities issued (120), and the net debt increases by 20.

Table A1.2 (concluded)

	Baseline: No Intervention	Issuing Guarantees (viii)	Assuming One-Off Debt Service of Guaranteed Debt (ix)		Servicing Debt When Guarantee Is Called (x)	
			With creating an effective claim on defaulter (ix)a	Without creating an effective claim on defaulter (ix)b	With creating an effective claim on defaulter (x)a	Without creating an effective claim on defaulter (x)b
(1) Revenue	150	150	150	150	152	150
Of which interest received	0	0	0	0	2	0
(2) Expense	100	100	100	111	100	205
Of which interest	0	0	0	0	0	5
Of which capital transfers	0	0	0	11	0	100
(3) = (1) – (2) Net/gross operating balance	50	50	50	39	52	–55
(4) Net acquisition of nonfinancial assets	50	50	50	50	50	50
(5) = (3) – (4) also = (6) Net lending/borrowing	0	0	0	–11	2	–105
(6) = (7) – (8) Transactions in financial assets and liabilities (financing)	0	0	0	–11	2	–105
(7) Net acquisition of financial assets	0	0	11	0	2	–105
Of which						
Currency and deposits	0	0	0	0	–98	–105
(7.1) Loans for policy purposes	0	0	11	0	100	0
(8) Net incurrence of liabilities	0	0	11	11	0	0
Of which						
Securities other than shares	0	0	0	0	0	0
Loans	0	0	11	11	0	0
(9) = (5) – (7.1) Overall balance	0	0	–11	–11	–98	0
Memorandum item: Outstanding guarantees	0	1000	990	990	900	900

Assume: Interest on government securities issued: 5 percent; interest earned on assets acquired by government: 2 percent; and interest on cash deposits of government: 0 percent.

Government assistance through guarantees

(viii) Government provides support to the industry by issuing guarantees to the total amount of 1,000.

This issuance of guarantees does not affect the net worth of government because the transaction is not recorded in the operation of government. Government's stock of gross, and net, debt remains unchanged because such guarantees are not regarded as government liabilities until such time as these are called. However, for transparency purposes, record the total outstanding amount of guarantees as a memorandum item on the government accounts.

(ix)a Government assumes the obligation to service a one-off principal (10) and interest (1) payment that was guaranteed due to temporary liquidity constraint of a bank.

This exchange of one type of asset for another has no primary impact on net worth of government. Since the bank remains a going concern, government acquires an effective claim on the bank. The secondary impact of interest receivable increases net worth of government to the extent that it is more than interest forgone on the cash deposit. The implied "cost" of the assistance is potential losses on the assets acquired. Government's stock of gross debt increases and net debt remains unchanged.

(ix)b Government assumes the obligation to service a principal (10) and interest payment (1) that was guaranteed, but due to fundamental insolvency issues, government does not obtain an effective claim on the defaulter bank.

The assumption of this obligation directly reduces net worth of government due to the capital transfer. In addition, net worth could also decrease to the extent that revenue reduces due to interest forgone on the cash deposits. Government's stocks of gross debt and net debt increase by 11.

(x)a A guarantee to the value of 100 is called. The defaulting bank is being restructured and government obtains an effective claim on the bank.

This exchange of one type of asset for another has no primary impact on net worth of government. Since the bank remains a going concern, government acquires an effective claim on the bank. The secondary impact of interest receivable increases net worth of government to the extent that it is more than interest forgone on the cash deposit. The implied "cost" of the assistance is potential losses on the assets acquired. Government's stock of gross, and net, debt remains unchanged, while the stock of outstanding guarantees reduces with the amount of the called guarantee.

(x)b A guarantee to the value of 100 is called. The defaulting bank is insolvent and government does not obtain an effective claim on the bank.

A called guarantee has the same impact as loan assumption, assuming the loan directly reduces net worth of government due to the capital transfer. The secondary impact is a further reduction in net worth due to the interest payable on the assumed loan. Government's stock of gross, and net, debt increases with value of assumed loan, while outstanding guarantees reduce with the same amount.

Contingent Liabilities

Guarantees by the government or the central bank represent a contingent liability and a potentially important fiscal cost. Usually, the cost of guarantees is recorded ex post when government honors the guarantee that is called. However, given the fiscal risks, it is important to disclose the contingent liability and include it in debt sustainability scenarios. Where a government charges for the provision of a guarantee (as is required under state aid rules of the European Union (EU)), the fee improves the government's operating balance.

- *Under statistical reporting standards* (*GFSM 2001* or the EU's *European System of Accounts 1995* (*ESA-95*)), contingent liabilities are not considered liabilities until the contingency materializes, and therefore they need not be recorded in financial statements as a liability/expense until then. Once the contingency has materialized and payments need to be made, the associated liabilities should be reported as in Tables A1.1 and A1.2, columns viii–x.[39] It should be noted that *GFSM 2001* asks for the disclosure of the value of contingencies in memorandum items. The IMF *Code of Good Practices on Fiscal Transparency* also calls for

statements as part of the budget documentation that describe the nature and significance of all contingent liabilities.

- *For accounting purposes*, the *International Public Sector Accounting Standards* for accrual accounting require disclosure in notes to financial statements of contractual contingent liabilities when the possibility of payment is "not remote."

- *Good disclosure practice* is to publish detailed information on guarantees. This should cover the public policy purpose of each guarantee or guarantee program, the total amount of the guarantee classified by sectors and duration, the intended beneficiaries, and likelihood the guarantee will be called. Information should also be provided on past calls of guarantees. Best practice would be to compute the expected value of the increase in government liabilities due to called guarantees. Implicit liabilities should generally not be disclosed to prevent moral hazard (see Cebotari, 2008).

- *Debt sustainability analysis* should cover all of the debt created by the restructuring operations, including quasifiscal interventions and various assumptions for contingent liabilities that may materialize. It should also present scenarios on recovery rates of debt repayments by recapitalized agencies, and resources generated from the sale of acquired assets and equity stakes.

---

[39]The 2008 System of National Accounts distinguishes between one-off guarantees and standardized guarantees. The former are recorded only when the guarantee is called, while for the latter the present value of expected calls (net of expected recoveries) is recorded.

Appendix II   Financial Sector Support Measures

This appendix provides a detailed summary of the financial sector support measures and their net costs in advanced and emerging market countries. The focus is on new special facilities rather than support through regular liquidity facilities. In addition to the specific measures announced or implemented in each country, it provides information on the potential magnitude of support, estimates of the upfront fiscal cost, and information on how countries currently propose to treat the different measures in their fiscal accounts (which is not in all cases consistent with the recommended treatment in Appendix I). Based on the analysis in Appendixes III and VI, the expected net costs of financial support operations (including recapitalization, purchase of assets, liquidity provision, and guarantees) are calculated in Tables A2.1 and A2.2.

The data have been compiled jointly with the IMF's Monetary and Capital Markets Department, relying primarily on information from official government sources, such as treasuries and central banks. These have been supplemented by information from financial market sources, including investment and commercial banks, ratings agencies, and private consultancy companies. Information by country is presented in Table A2.3. The figures reported reflect official announcements of amounts allocated for financial sector support, not necessarily actual disbursements.[40]

---

[40]In some instances, the amounts announced have not yet been formally committed through legislation or regulation.

Table A2.1. Upfront Gross Fiscal Cost and Estimated Recovery Rate
(In percent of GDP, unless otherwise indicated)

	Upfront Government Financing	Recovery Rate[1]		Medium-Term Net Cost of Direct Support	
		Point estimate	95% interval	Point estimate	95% interval
Average for[2]					
G-20 economies	3.6	48.0	[28.2, 67.7]	1.6	[0.9, 2.2]
Advanced economies	5.6	50.6	[29.5, 71.4]	2.4	[1.4, 3.4]
Emerging economies	0.4	35.3	[21.3, 49.2]	0.2	[0.1, 0.3]

Source: IMF staff estimates. See Appendix III for details.
[1]In percent of upfront outlays.
[2]Weighted by PPP GDP of 2007.

Table A2.2. Hypothetical Net Cost from Financial Sector Support Measures: Illustrative Scenarios

(In percent of GDP, unless otherwise indicated)

| | Net Cost of Direct Support (i) | Guarantees | | | New Special Facilities by Central Banks and Others[2] | | Total Net Cost (i)+(ii)+(iii) |
| | | | Expected cost[1] | | | | |
		Gross	Point estimate (ii)	Range	Gross	Net (iii)	
Average for[3]							
G-20 economies	1.6	8.8	1.0	[0.6, 2.0]	10.7	1.1	3.7
Advanced economies	2.4	14.0	1.7	[1.0, 3.2]	15.4	1.5	5.6
Emerging economies	0.2	0.1	0.0	[0.0, 0.0]	2.9	0.3	0.5

Source: IMF staff estimates.

[1]Cumulative cost over five years. Guarantee fees have not been netted from the gross cost of guarantees given the variability in fees across countries and maturity structure of debt, and given the legislative differences in applying those fees. The range reflects assumptions of (1) an optimistic recovery rate of 80 percent; and (2) a conservative recovery rate of 40 percent.

[2]The gross numbers for central bank support are based on announcements or commitments of new special facilities, and do not necessarily reflect actual outlays. The recovery rate is assumed to be 90 percent.

[3]Weighted by PPP GDP of 2007.

Table A2.3. Financial Sector Support Operations in Selected Countries
(As of May 2009; in local currencies, unless otherwise stated)

Program	Amount (billion)	Operations	Gross Treasury Financing Need	Reporting
Argentina				
Loans	9	Loans of Arg$1.7 billion to the agricultural sector; Arg$1.3 billion to the manufacturing sector; Arg$3.1 billion to those buying their first car; Arg$3.5 million to those buying home appliances; Arg$3 billion to SMEs; Arg$300 million for home refurbishing. All of these measures are likely to be financed by Anses (Administración Nacional de la Seguridad Social).	0	This operation will likely involve the transfer of Anses' deposits to a number of commercial banks. As Anses is not part of the central government, it will not be reflected in the central government accounts.
Total	9		0	
Australia				
Deposit insurance	…	Government will guarantee all deposits (no explicit deposit insurance before).	0	The deposit guarantee was reported as a contingent liability in the Statement of Risks in the Mid-Year Economic and Fiscal Outlook (MYEFO). If the guarantee is called upon it will be paid by the government and reported as an expenditure (likely as a capital transfer).
Guarantee	104	Government will guarantee, for a fee, eligible wholesale borrowing (new and existing term issuance up to five years) of Australian-owned banks, Australian subsidiaries of foreign banks, and credit unions.	0	The wholesale funding guarantee was reported as a contingent liability in the Statement of Risks in MYEFO. To the extent that the guarantee is quantifiable in future, those values will be detailed as a "quantifiable contingent liability." If the guarantee is called upon it will be paid by the Treasury portfolio and will be reported as an expenditure.
Purchase of assets	8	Purchase of up to $A 4 billion of residential mortgage-backed securities (RMBS) from institutions that are not eligible for guarantee. The Australian Office of Financial Management has been directed to purchase another $A 4 billion of RMBS from nonauthorized deposit-taking institutions, in addition to the $A 4 billion already announced.	8	These purchases of AAA-rated RMBS will be reported as financing (purchases of financial assets).
Total	112		8	
Austria				
Deposit insurance	10	Unlimited deposit insurance by the end of 2009. The government committed €10 billion to back this scheme.	10	Government guarantee. Not expected to be reported.
Guarantee	75	€75 billion is pledged to guarantee the interbank market, of which €10 billion for a medium-term interbank clearing facility.	0	Government guarantee. Not expected to be reported.
Capital injection	15	€15 billion is pledged for bank recapitalization. As of mid-April 2009, €4.65 billion has actually been used.	15	Will be reported in the government accounts as financing (purchase of financial assets).
Total	100		25	
Belgium				
Guarantee	91	Two types of guarantees: (1) a guarantee by the government to the National Bank extending collateralized loans to banks; and (2) new interbank and institutional deposits and financing as well as new bond issuance intended for institutional investments by a number of Dexia entities. €90 billion for Dexia, the rest is unallocated.	0	Government guarantees. Not expected to be reported.

Measure		Description		Notes
Capital injection	16	Dexia (€2 billion), Fortis (€9.4 billion), KBC Group (€3.5 billion), and Ethias (€1.5 billion).	16	Will be reported in the government accounts as financing (purchase of financial assets).
Total	107		16	
Brazil				
Crisis Liquidity Facilities	53	Central bank (BCB) initiated repo operations in dollars. Loans outstanding as of December 23, 2008 were US$13.9 billion (0.9 percent of GDP) having peaked at US$14.9 billion. Most expiring contracts are being rolled over. Central bank announced dollar lending program for up to US$10 billion (0.6 percent of GDP)—amounts will be lent to banks with commitment to on-lend to firms amortizing foreign debts. This facility has not been used by June 2009.	0	Primarily implemented by the central bank, these measures will not be reported in the government accounts.
Central bank liquidity support	99	Central bank support measures in Brazil included targeted easing of reserve requirements intended to boost liquidity in institutions most affected by the crisis. These measures accounted for an increase of R$98.9 billion in systemic liquidity.	0	Central bank operations.
Direct liquidity support	23	Public banks (Banco do Brasil and Nossa Caixa) announced credit lines totaling up to R$8 billion a piece to purchase loan portfolio from small banks. Deposit insurance fund purchases CDs and some other obligations issued by smaller banks for R$15 billion. Of this, R$2.5 billion had been used as of December 17, 2008.	0	Implemented by public banks, this measure will not be reported in the government accounts.
Total	174		0	
Canada				
Purchase of assets	135	Canada Mortgage and Housing Corporation will purchase up to Can$135 billion of insured mortgage. Purchase of Can$56.6 billion has been completed by mid-May, with up to Can$70 billion available in the first half of the 2009/10 fiscal year.	135	The corporation is a public corporation (owned by the government). These purchases are therefore directly reported in the government accounts.
Liquidity	24	Crisis Liquidity Facilities. Increased the size of term purchase and resale agreements (PRAs) to around US$25 billion (1.9 percent of GDP). A PRA is an arrangement between the Bank of Canada and dealers whereby the Bank buys treasuries from a dealer, and the dealer agrees to repurchase the treasuries the next day.	0	Central bank operation, not reported in the government accounts.
Loan by Treasury to auto makers	14	The Canadian government, together with the Government of Ontario, has provided Chrysler and General Motors with loans.	14	Reported as financing.
Credit facility	12	Canadian Secured Credit Facility has been newly established. The budget sets aside Can$12 billion to purchase securities backed by loans and leases on vehicles and equipment.	12	The purchases will be reported directly, since they will be undertaken by the Business Development Bank of Canada—a crown corporation.
Guarantee	216	The government created the Canadian Lender's Assurance Facility which provides insurance on the wholesale term borrowing of deposit taking institutions (so far, there have been no requests for such guarantees). A new Canadian Life Insurers Assurance Facility has been announced, to guarantee insurers' wholesale term borrowing. The Canadian government now guarantees the warranties of new vehicles purchased from General Motors of Canada and Chrysler Canada Inc. (Can$0.2 billion).	0	Government guarantees. Not expected to be reported.

Table A2.3 (continued)

Program	Amount (billion)	Operations	Gross Treasury Financing Need	Reporting
Support to crown corporations	13	The government increased the authorized capital limits of Export Development Corporation (EDC) and Business Development Bank of Canada (BDC), increased EDC's contingent liability limit to Can$45 billion, and increased Canadian Deposit Insurance Corporation's borrowing limit by Can$9 billion.	13	The corporations are public corporations (owned by the government). These transactions would be reported in the government accounts.
Total	414		174	
China				
Capital injection	3	Capital injection to Chinese airline companies.	3	This operation will involve the sale of newly issued stocks to the airlines' state-owned parent companies. They will therefore not be reported in the government accounts.
Total	3		3	
France				
Capital injection	27	€3 billion for Dexia, of which €2 billion from Caisse des Dépôts et Consignations (CDC) and €21 billion for others. Additional €3 billion is available from the merger between Groupe des Banques Populaires and Groupe des Caisses d'Epargne.	25	Will be reported in the government accounts below the line as financing (purchase of financial assets).
Bank lending guarantee	320	Up to €320 billion will be made available to guarantee bank lending.	0	Government guarantee. Not expected to be reported.
Corporate loan	26	Government has announced a fund of €20 billion to support the country's strategic companies. The government will raise €6 billion, with the rest coming from a state-owned bank, CDC. Government has extended more credit to PSA Peugeot Citroën and Renault SA and said aid to the carmakers may reach €6 billion in return for their pledges to keep domestic plants open.	6	The authorities have reported €3 billion in the budget as expenditure and it is unclear how the remainder of the fund contribution will be accounted for. The modalities of the €6 billion credit having yet to be specified, the way this credit will be reported in the government's account also remains unclear.
Total	373		31	
Germany				
Deposit insurance	...	Public commitment by government to fully cover household deposits.	0	Is not expected to be reported in the government accounts.
Capital injection	91	€10 billion for Bayern LB, €1.358 billion for IKB, and €80 billion for other bank recapitalization.	91	Will be reported in the government accounts as financing (purchase of financial assets).
Asset purchase	10	Stabilization fund to provide €10 billion for purchase of troubled assets.	0	The stabilization fund is not part of the government.
Debt guarantee	438	Stabilization fund provides interbank loan guarantees (€400 billion). It is expected that 5 percent of guaranteed amount may be called upon. €23 billion for West LB and €15 billion for Hypo real estate.	0	The stabilization fund is not part of the government.
Capital injection	3	Two German states, Hamburg and Schleswig-Holstein, will inject €3 billion capital into HSH Nordbank.	0	Capital injection projected by local governments.
Guarantee	10	Two German states, Hamburg and Schleswig-Holstein, have agreed to guarantee up to €10 billion to cover future losses arising from HSH Nordbank.	0	Guarantees provided by local governments.
Total	552		91	

Greece

Measure	Amount	Description	Reporting treatment	Value
Deposit insurance	...	Deposit insurance up to €100,000 for all deposits.	The fund guaranteeing the deposits is not part of the government. These guarantees are not expected to be reported as a contingent liability.	0
Capital injection	5	Government announced €28 billion rescue plan. The plan permits the injection of up to €5 billion for bank capital in the form of preferred shares. The shareholders of Alpha Bank approved the government's capital injection of €940 million in preference shares. The shareholders of Eurobank approved the government's capital injection of €345.5 million in preference shares. (These are under a package of €5 billion.)	Will be reported in the government accounts as financing (purchase of financial assets). Preferred shares will pay a fixed annual return of 20 percent, which will be reported as revenue.	5
Loan guarantee	15	Government backs new loans up to €15 billion.	Expected to be reflected as a contingent liability. Related fees will be reported as a revenue.	0
Lending	8	Issuance of up to €8 billion in special bonds to boost bank liquidity. The bonds will be lent directly to the banks at their nominal value against payment of a fee plus collateral.	Could be reported under the line as collateralized loan. Related fees will be reported as a revenue.	8
Total	28			13

Hungary

Measure	Amount	Description	Reporting treatment	Value
Deposit insurance	...	Increase in deposit insurance to Ft 13 million.	Expected to be reported as a contingent liability.	0
Liquidity provision	1,881	ECB repo facility €5 billion. In addition, regulations are changed to allow pension funds to invest all of their funds into government bonds.	Central bank operation, not reported in the government accounts.	0
Liquidity provision	644	The government has committed a direct lending of €2.3 billion to three banks.	Will be reported as financing.	644
Capital injection	300	Hungary is trying to set aside Ft 600 billion for banking sector—half to enhance banks' capital ratios and half to guarantee interbank lending.	A fund will be created for that purpose. The fund will be capitalized though a government transfer, which is expected to be reported in the government accounts as financing. Any capital injection is expected to be reported in the fund accounts as financing (purchase of financial assets).	300
Guarantee	300	Interbank lending.	Another fund will be created for that purpose. The fund will be capitalized though a government transfer, which is expected to be reported as financing. The cost of called guarantees will be reported as transfers in the fund accounts. These funds are not expected to be consolidated in the general government accounts.	0
Total	3,125			944

India

Measure	Amount	Description	Reporting treatment	Value
Liquidity provision	4,228	Crisis liquidity facility including measures taken in January 2009.	Central bank operation, not reported in the government accounts.	0
Capital injection	200	Bank recapitalization.	Will be reported in the government accounts as financing—borrowing and drawdown of Treasury deposits.	200
Total	4,428			200

Indonesia

Measure	Amount	Description	Reporting treatment	Value
Guarantee	4,000	Export financing agency will be running within nine months and will provide guarantees, insurance, or lending. The agency will be housed under the Ministry of Finance and will have initial capital of Rp 4 trillion.	The transfer of capital will be reported in the government budget as financing.	4,000
Total	4,000			4,000

Table A2.3 (continued)

Program	Amount (billion)	Operations	Gross Treasury Financing Need	Reporting
Ireland				
Deposit insurance	368	Deposit insurance increased to unlimited for all deposits (retail, commercial, institutional, and interbank), covered bonds, senior debt, and dated subordinated debt of Irish banks and deposit institutions.	0	The insurance is provided by the government. The corresponding contingent liability is not expected to be reported.
Capital injection	11	Recapitalization program for credit institutions. Part of the funds will come from the National Pensions Reserve Fund. The state's investment will take the form of preference shares and/or ordinary shares and the state may where appropriate participate on an underwriting basis. A recapitalization plan of €7 billion was announced for the Allied Irish Bank and Bank of Ireland, funded by the existing allocation for recapitalization.	11	The government's investment will be reported in the government accounts as financing (purchase of financial assets).
Purchase of assets	...	The government outlined plans to set up a national asset management agency to take over an estimated €80–90 billion of bad loans extended by local domestic banks to developers and property companies. The government's plan is to remove all land and property development loans from the banks' balance sheets and replace them with government bonds. The amount paid by the agency will be significantly less than the book value to take account of the agency's estimation of the worth of the loans, to compensate the state for taking on these risks, and the banks that will have to take the associated losses. Should losses be incurred by the agency over a 10 to 15 years timeframe, the government intends that a levy should be applied to recoup any shortfall.	...	Will be reported in the government accounts as financing—borrowing and drawdown of Treasury deposit.
Total	379		11	
Italy				
Guarantee	...	Ministry of Finance authorized to guarantee loans granted by the Bank of Italy to banks; issue a state guarantee to back up the Italian interbank deposit insurance, up to €103,191.38; and issue a state guarantee for new Italian bank liabilities with maturity of less than five years.	0	These guarantees are expected to be reported as other contingent liabilities in an annex to the budget law.
Recapitalization	11	The recapitalization measures were provided to subscribe subordinated debt instruments (to be counted as bank core tier 1 capital). The budget for these measures will be around €10–12 billion.	11	Reported in the government accounts as financing (purchase of financial assets).
Liquidity swap	40	Provide for temporary exchanges of government securities held by the central bank with assets held by Italian banks.	0	Central bank operation, not reported in the government accounts.
Total	51		11	
Japan				
Guarantee	37,000	Ministry of Finance provides a ¥33 trillion package (with ¥900 billion budget support) through the policy-based financing institutions to the SMEs, including a government guarantee of ¥20 trillion. Additional support of ¥41.8 trillion was announced in April 2009. The government will provide ¥3 trillion for the new measures. Additional guarantees of ¥17 trillion were identified.	3,900	Credit guarantees are not expected to be reported in the budget. The ¥3.9 trillion that the government will inject into policy-based financing institutions (including Japan Finance Corporation) for them to finance the lending and guarantees will be reported in the government accounts as spending.

Measure	Amount		Description
Lending and purchase of commercial papers (CPs)	37,800	0	Ministry of Finance provides a ¥33 trillion package through the policy-based financing institutions to the SMEs, including loans of ¥11 trillion and purchase of CPs of ¥2 trillion. The additional support of ¥41.8 trillion announced in April 2009 includes a variety of liquidity measures, which is assumed to amount to ¥24.8 trillion.
Capital injection	12,000	0	A special corporation will participate in commercial banks for up to ¥12 trillion.
Purchase of assets	1,000	0	The Bank of Japan announced that it will resume a program of stock purchases. The Bank will purchase ¥1 trillion worth of stocks held by financial institutions. The purchase will be financed by the Bank.
Purchase of corporate bond	1,000	0	The Bank of Japan announced a purchase of corporate bonds up to ¥1 trillion.
Purchase of commercial banks' stock holdings	20,000	0	A special corporation could buy up to ¥20 trillion in stocks from the commercial banks.
Purchase of assets	50,000	0	A special corporation could buy up to ¥50 trillion in stocks from the market. The government provides guarantees for the financing.
Purchase of CP	5,000	0	The Bank of Japan established "Principal Terms and Conditions for Outright Purchases of CP", with the aim of ensuring stability in financial markets as well as facilitating corporate financing by conducting appropriate money market operations.
Total	**163,800**	**3,900**	
Korea			
Guarantee	148,000		Guarantee to Korean banks' external debt issued until end-2009 for three years (capped at $100 billion). W 18 trillion has also been provided to increase the credit guarantee fund.
Purchase of assets	16,300		Creation of a W 10 trillion fund to purchase bonds and commercial papers issued by SMEs and corporations. State-run Korea Asset Management to purchase up to $900 million of construction loans from savings banks (W 1.3 trillion). No direct government funding is expected. The government also announced a W 5 trillion purchase of unsold houses, of which W 1.5 trillion has been used by June 2009.
Liquidity support	2,500		Central bank expanded the lending facility (with a low interest rate) for SMEs by W 2.5 trillion (total W 9 trillion).
Bank recapitalization	20,000		Creation of a W 20 trillion fund to purchase commercial banks' preferred stocks, hybrid bonds, and subordinated debt to augment the banks' capital.
Capital injection	3,950		In-kind investment in public financial institutions (W 1.85 trillion) in 2008. Cash injection into eight state-run financial institutions to support lending to SMEs and exporting firms (W 3.51 trillion) in the 2009 budget.
Purchase of assets	40,000		The government announced that its state-owned Korea Asset Management Company will issue W 40 trillion of government-guaranteed bonds to purchase nonperforming loans—troubled assets of financial institutions and companies under restructuring. The fund will be in operation until 2014. The bills proposing these initiatives were submitted to the National Assembly in April 2009.
Total	**230,750**	**8,010**	

Descriptions (middle-column notes for Japan items, in order): The corporation will finance its purchases by borrowing, with a government guarantee. / Central bank operation, not reported in the government accounts. / Central bank operation, not reported in the government accounts. / The corporation will finance its purchases by borrowing, with a government guarantee. / The corporation will finance its purchases by borrowing, with a government guarantee. / Central bank operation, not reported in the government accounts.

Descriptions (Korea notes): These guarantees will be provided by the Ministry of Strategy and Finance and reported as government's contingent liabilities. / This fund will be funded by the central bank, the Korea Development Bank, and institutional banks. The purchases will therefore not be reported directly in the government accounts. / Central bank operation, not reported in the government accounts. / This fund will be funded by the central bank, the Korea Development Bank, and institutional banks. The purchases will therefore not be reported directly in the government accounts. / The injection of equity will be provided by the government. Expected to be reported as spending (transfers). / The purchase will not be reported directly in the government accounts, while the guarantees will be recorded as government's contingent liabilities.

Table A2.3 (continued)

Program	Amount (billion)	Operations	Gross Treasury Financing Need	Reporting
Netherlands				
Deposit insurance	...	Up to €100,000 for one year for all deposits.	0	The insurance is covered by the banks and the central bank and is therefore not recorded in the government accounts.
Loan guarantee	200	Conditional guarantees for loan between banks and institutional investors. €200 billion is allocated for this facility, but the amount actually used by end-2008 is very limited.	0	These government guarantees will be mentioned in the budget documents but no quantitative estimates are expected to be provided.
Purchase of assets	17	The government purchased €16.8 billion equity from Fortis Holding in Belgium to nationalize Fortis Netherlands.	17	Will be reported in the government accounts as financing (purchase of assets).
Capital injection	20	ING (€10 billion) and €10 billion is available for other banks. The actual capital injection by June 2009 was €13.8 billion.	20	Will be reported in the government accounts as financing (purchase of financial assets).
Loans	44	To ensure financial stability and continuity of the activities of Fortis in the Netherlands, the state took over the bank and provided a bridging loan of €44.341 billion. The loan will be repaid in 2009, but is still outstanding as of May 2009.	44	Will be reported in the government accounts as financing.
Total	281		81	
Norway				
Capital injection/ liquidity swap	350	The Storting (Norwegian parliament) has authorized the Ministry of Finance to exchange with banks government securities against collateral in or in return for Norwegian covered bonds in amounts up to a total of NKr 350 billion. It is a swap arrangement with conservative haircuts, and less than half of the announced amount has been used so far.	350	Will be reported in the government accounts as financing.
Recapitalization	50	The Government proposes the establishment of the State Finance Fund. The purpose for this Fund will be to provide tier I capital to financially sound Norwegian banks in order to strengthen the banks' core capital and to improve their lending capacity. The State Finance Fund will be established as a separate legal entity, with NKr 50 billion in capital. In line with the fiscal guidelines, this operation will be covered by borrowing in the market and/or drawing on the Treasury's cash reserves (50 percent borrowing is assumed).	25	Will be reported in the government accounts as financing—borrowing and drawdown of Treasury deposits.
Purchase of assets	50	The Norwegian government has proposed a new NKr 50 billion fund to boost bank capital and invest in the corporate bond market. In line with the fiscal guidelines, this operation will be covered by borrowing in the market and/or drawing on the Treasury's cash reserves (50 percent borrowing is assumed).	25	Will be reported in the government accounts as financing—borrowing and drawdown of Treasury deposits.
Total	450		400	
Poland				
Guarantees	40	The government will provide guarantees for interbank lending up to Zl 40 billion, if needed.	0	This guarantee is provided directly by the government and will be reported in its accounts as a contingent liability.
Deposit insurance	...	The Bank Guarantee Fund law has been amended to increase the level of deposit guarantee from €22,500 to €50,000 and eliminate coinsurance.	...	Is not expected to be reported in the government accounts.

Measure	Amount	Description	Reported	Comment
Liquidity provision	...	National Bank of Poland provides a variety of liquidity support, including (i) weekly three-month (and six-month from May) repo operations; (ii) broadening of the range of collateral and reduced haircuts for Lombard credit; (iii) euro swaps with domestic banks; and (iv) a repo line with the ECB up to €10 billion. However, these measures are difficult to quantify.		Central bank operations.
Total	40		0	
Portugal				
Deposit insurance	...	Formal deposit insurance increased to €100,000.	0	Government guarantee. Not expected to be reported.
Guarantee	20	A special scheme provides guarantees to credit institutions, available for the renewal of financing operations. A maximum amount of €20 billion is allocated to both guarantees and capital injection, with the latter not exceeding €4 billion.	0	Government guarantee. Not expected to be reported.
Capital injection	4	Government will make €4 billion available to banks seeking to strengthen their capital.	4	Will be reported in the government accounts as financing (purchase of financial assets).
Total	20		4	
Russia				
Deposit insurance	200	Government will widen remit of deposit insurance agency by injecting Rub 200 billion from the budget.	200	The recapitalization of the agency by the government is reported above the line as a transfer. The insurance is not reported as a contingent liability.
Purchase of assets	200	Purchase of mortgages from banks up to Rub 200 billion. Financed from the National Welfare Fund.	0	This operation will not be reported in the government accounts.
Capital injection	505	Government capital injection in the State Mortgage Agency amounts to Rub 60 billion in the 2008 supplementary budget and Rub 20 billion in the 2009 supplementary budget. Public capital has also been injected into VEB: Rub 75 billion in the 2008 supplementary budget and Rub 100 billion in the 2009 supplementary budget.	505	All transactions reported in the 2008 and 2009 supplementary budgets.
Central bank lending	1,496	The central bank's new uncollateralized lending facility on top of Rub 200 billion rolled over via daily repos has eased local liquidity. As of May 2009, Rub 1,053 billion has been provided. The central bank also provided other loans of Rub 850 billion (against nontraded collateral).	0	Central bank operation, not reported in the government accounts.
Bank loan/Recapitalization	1,787	Subordinated loans to VTB, Sberbank, Rosselkhozbank, and others; some of the. injections were through VEB and the central bank. Collateralized lending of $6.5 billion to Alfa group and RusAl (financed from foreign reserves).	250	Central bank operation (in coordination with VEB). Of the total, Rub 180 billion to VTB; Rub 45 billion to Rosselkhozbank and Rub 25 billion to Rosagroleasing are reported in the government accounts as part of the 2009 supplementary budget.
Liquidity support	300	Government deposit to commercial banks with an interest rate of U.S. dollar LIBOR + 1 percent.	0	Central bank operation, not reported in the government accounts.
Total	4,488		955	
Saudi Arabia				
Liquidity provision	11	Government has deposited up to US$3 billion to local banks to meet a shortfall of dollar funding in the domestic banking sector.	11	This deposit will be reported as financing.
Loan	10	"No-fee" loan from the government to Saudi citizens through the Saudi Credit Bank ($2.7 billion).	10	The government contribution will be reported as spending (transfer).

Table A2.3 (continued)

Program	Amount (billion)	Operations	Gross Treasury Financing Need	Reporting
Guarantee	...	The supreme economic council has offered guarantees for all bank deposits.	0	The corresponding contingent liability is not expected to be reported.
Other support	...	In order to restore liquidity to the banking system which has now normalized, several government agencies placed long-term deposits in the banking system. The Public Investment Fund increased its level of co-participation in financing with local banks, and extended the term (from 15–20 years), loan ceiling, and grace period (to 5 years). These are difficult to quantify.	...	
Total	21		21	
Spain				
Deposit insurance	...	Deposit insurance increased to €100,000.	0	Government guarantee. Not expected to be reported.
Guarantee	200	Cabinet approved plans to guarantee up to €100 billion of bank debt for 2009. Another €100 billion of guarantees can be extended, if needed.	0	Government guarantee. Not expected to be reported.
Purchase of assets	50	Government announced plans to set up a fund up to €50 billion to buy nontoxic assets from banks and other financial institutions. Initial endowment of €30 billion could be expanded to €50 billion.	50	The fund will be part of the government. The purchases will be reported in the government accounts as financing (purchases of financial assets).
Total	250		50	
Sweden				
Deposit guarantee	0	Bank deposit guarantee for all types of accounts of private and legal persons up to SKr 500,000. Deposit insurance fund has SKr 18 billion.	0	While the government is the ultimate guarantor of the Deposit Guarantee Scheme, which had SKr 17 billion of reserves in early October 2008, the corresponding contingent liabilities are not expected to be reported.
Guarantee	1,500	The state will initially guarantee up to SKr 1,500 billion of debt instruments, including bonds, certificates of deposits, and other nonsubordinated debt. However, this scheme has not yet found acceptance within the banking sector and is likely to be revised in order to make it acceptable. By end-May 2009, guarantees of about SKr 300 billion have been provided.	0	This scheme aims at ensuring the rollover of banks' existing debt instruments of more than 90 days' maturity: in exchange for a market-based fee charged by the government to an applicant bank, the former agrees to guarantee the latter's refinanced debt obligations. The fees will be reported above the line as revenue. It is unclear whether the corresponding contingent liabilities will be reported.
Liquidity support from Swedish National Debt Office (SNDO)	150	Starting mid-September 2008, the SNDO issued SKr 150 billion worth of short-term treasury bills to use the proceeds to inject funds into the mortgage securities market via reverse repos.	150	Reported in government accounts as financing operation.
Liquidity support from Riksbank	487	Riksbank programs: up to SKr 180 billion lent through three- and six-month kronor lending program; up to $35 billion to ease U.S. dollar shortage in the 30–90 day spectrum; SKr 75 billion through the Riksbank Certificated program; SKr 8 billion through the CP program. Special liquidity assistance to Kaupthing's Swedish subsidiary of SKr 5 billion on October 8, 2008.	0	Central bank operation, not reported in the government accounts.

Capital injection	65	A stabilization fund will be set up to manage potential solvency problems, where the government will contribute SKr 15 billion. Sweden announced additional plans to inject up to SKr 50 billion into its financial sector. This new program will be financed from the stability fund presented in October 2008. The Swedish government stated that it may buy as much as 70 percent of new shares and hybrid capital from banks. Banks receiving a capital injection will be required to freeze bonus payments and wage increases for executives for two years.	15	The modalities of the fund having yet to be specified, the way the government's contribution will be reported on the government's account remains unclear.
Total	2,202		165	
Switzerland				
Purchase of illiquid assets	42	Swiss National Bank provided $35 billion and UBS contributed $4 billion to a Special Purpose Vehicle, which acquires illiquid assets from the bank.	0	Central bank operation, not reported in the government accounts.
Deposit insurance	...	Plan to raise deposit insurance for private customers from Sw F 30,000 (amount not decided yet).	0	Expected to be privately run. Not reported in the government accounts.
Capital injection	6	Purchase of convertible notes, to be redeemed or converted within 30 months.	6	Expected to be reported as spending (capital expenditure).
Total	48		6	
Turkey				
Liquidity provision	0	Financed by the governmental Agency for Developing and Supporting SMEs (KOSGEB) and with intermediation of 7 banks, a total of YTL 350 million of financing will be extended to manufacturer tradesmen, artisans, and SMEs at a zero interest rate with size of financing being dependent on the number of existing employees (up to YTL 100,000).	0	Will not be reported in the government accounts.
Liquidity provision	3	A loan of $1.65 billion was provided to SME exporters by KOSGEB.	0	Will not be reported in the government accounts.
Other support	...	Under a protocol signed between Turkish Union of Chambers and Commodity Exchanges (TOBB) and Halkbank (a state-owned bank), union member SMEs can use loans with low interest rates. Under a protocol signed between Turkish Textile Employers' Association and Ziraat Bank (a state-owned bank), association members can use loans with low interest rates. These are difficult to quantify.	...	
Total	3		0	
United Kingdom				
Deposit insurance	...	100 percent up to £50,000.	...	May be reported as contingent liabilities
Credit guarantee scheme	250	The government guarantees short- to medium-term debt issuance to meet maturing funding needs (estimated at £250 billion), extended until December 2009.	0	The corresponding contingent liabilities will be reported in the long-term public finance report, to be published with the 2009 budget.
Bank recapitalization fund	56	The government injected £20 billion for Royal Bank of Scotland (RBS) and £17 billion for Lloyds/HBOS in 2008. Additional £19 billion has been provided for RBS in March 2009 (£13 billion of capital injection and £6 billion of an option, which is highly expected to be exercised soon). The actual support provided by March 2009 is £6 billion more than the maximum amount committed in 2008 (£50 billion).	56	Will be done through the purchase of preferred shares and common stock and reported as financing (purchase of financial assets).

Table A2.3 (*continued*)

Program	Amount (billion)	Operations	Gross Treasury Financing Need	Reporting
Special liquidity scheme	185	Bank of England swaps a variety of banks' less liquid assets for treasury bills. The window was closed down at end-January 2009. The amount drawn down is £185 billion. The outstanding amount is expected to be close to the total amount drawn down, given the three-year swap maturity.	185	Central bank operation, not reported in government accounts. The treasury bills issued for this swap are not expected to be included in government debt statistics, however, a final ruling of the Office for National Statistics is still pending.
Asset purchase facility	50	The Bank of England will set up and operate the U.K. Asset Purchase Facility to buy up to £50 billion of "high quality private sector assets." The Bank will focus initially on purchases of corporate bonds, commercial papers, and paper issued under the Credit Guarantee Scheme. The facility will be financed by the issue of treasury bills and the Debt Management Office's cash management operations. It appears that initially all £50 billion will be financed through extending central bank balance sheet. The Bank was given authorization to use the Asset Purchase Facility to buy up to £150 billion of assets financed by central bank money including gilts. Up to £50 billion will be used to purchase private sector assets. The Bank will also buy up to £100 billion of gilts.	0	Central bank operation, reported in both sides of the government accounts.
Working capital scheme and enterprise finance guarantee	11	The Working Capital Scheme is a direct response to the constraint on bank credit available for lending to ordinary-risk businesses with a turnover of up to £500 million a year. The Government will provide banks with guarantees covering 50 percent of the risk on existing and new working capital portfolios worth up to £20 billion. The Enterprise Finance Guarantee aims to help smaller, creditworthy companies that might otherwise fail to access the finance they need for working capital or investment finance due to the current tight lending conditions. The Government will also provide £1 billion of guarantees to support up to £1.3 billion of bank lending to smaller firms with an annual turnover of up to £25 million, which are looking for loans of up to £1 million for a period of up to 10 years.	0	The corresponding contingent liabilities will be reported in the long-term public finance report, to be published with the 2009 budget.
Asset protection scheme with RBS	254	The government launched a scheme to insure more than £500 billion of bank assets. The Asset Protection Scheme (APS) will run for a minimum five years. The first agreement under the APS was announced on February 26, 2009, covering £325 billion in RBS assets. The scheme serves to insure banks against large further losses on troubled assets, by limiting their exposure to the losses. According to the agreement, RBS will bear the initial loss up to 6 percent of the par value (£19.5 billion), on top of existing write-downs (£23 billion), and 10 percent of any additional shortfall. Therefore, the total guarantees provided by Treasury is £254.25 billion. In return, RBS committed to pay a 2 percent guarantee fee (in the form of nonvoting B shares) and forgo tax credit. Further, RBS made 2009 lending commitments totaling £25 billion: £9 billion of mortgage lending and £16 billion of business lending. It is likely that Lloyds will follow, and it seems that Treasury may need to expand this scheme.	0	The corresponding contingent liabilities will be reported in long-term public finance report, to be published with the 2009 budget. Calls on the guarantee would be reported as spending (capital transfer) and reported to parliament. It is unclear whether the guarantee fee will be reported on the government accounts or on the accounts of the state-owned company that manages government's financial sector participation (U.K. Financial Investments Limited). In either case, one way to do it would be to report the fee as revenue and financing (purchase of financial assets, in this case of nonvoting B shares in the financial institution).

Asset protection scheme with Lloyds	202	Lloyds will place £260 billion of assets into the Asset Protection Scheme, focusing on those assets with the greatest degree of uncertainty about their future performance. Lloyds will pay a participation fee of £15.6 billion to the Treasury in capital. The agreement will mean that in the event of a loss, Lloyds will bear a first loss amount after existing impairments of up to £25 billion. In return, Lloyds will make additional lending commitments totaling £3 billion of mortgage lending and £11 billion of business lending over the next 12 months. A similar lending commitment has been made in respect of the subsequent 12 months but this will be reviewed to ensure it reflects economic circumstances at that time.	0	The corresponding contingent liabilities will be reported in long-term public finance report, to be published with the 2009 budget. Calls on the guarantee would be reported as spending (capital transfer) and reported to parliament. It is unclear whether the guarantee fee will be reported on the government accounts or on the accounts of the state-owned company that manages government's financial sector participation (U.K. Financial Investments Limited). In either case, one way to do it would be to report the fee as revenue and financing (purchase of financial assets, in this case of nonvoting B shares in the financial institution).
Bank loan	149	Initial liquidity support of £99 billion (Northern Rock) and £50 billion (Bradford & Bingley) from the Bank of England. The 2008 PBR projects the loan for Northern Rock to be reduced to £14 billion at end-March 2009, and puts the cost of Bradford & Bingley at £18.2 billion.	48	Northern Rock and Bradford & Bingley (as well as RBS and HBOS) are now classified as public sector financial corporations, and their liabilities and short-term financial assets count toward public sector net debt. In the budget, authorities also report public sector net debt excluding financial sector interventions.
Total	1,158		289	
United States				
Recapitalization				
I. TARP				
Capital Purchase Program (CPP)	218	Treasury purchases of bank preferred shares, in return for dividend payments and warrants. Treasury's public commitment under the TARP umbrella amounts to $218 billion. Through mid-June 2009, the Treasury had purchased about $199 billion in preferred shares, of which $70 billion had been repaid by issuing institutions.	218	The Treasury and Office of Management and Budget (OMB) report the estimated subsidy element of the purchases as spending, with the rest being reported as financing (purchases of financial assets). The Congressional Budget Office (CBO) estimated the subsidy component of the $129 billion in outstanding purchases at $24 billion as of mid-June. Any losses to be incurred by the government would be reported above the line.
Support to Systemically Important Failing institutions (AIG)	70	$40 billion of equity injection in November 2008, plus announcement in March 2009 of a new equity capital facility that allows AIG to draw down up to $30 billion as needed over time in exchange for preferred stock to the U.S. Treasury (outstanding total purchases were approximately $41 billion by mid-June 2009).	70	See the reporting description for the CPP. The subsidy component of the transactions has been projected by CBO as $35 billion for the $70 billion in purchases outstanding as of mid-June. Any losses to be incurred by the government would be reported above the line.
Targeted Investment Program	40	Capital injections to Citigroup and Bank of America, $20 billion each.	40	See the reporting description for the CPP. The subsidy component of the $20 billion injected to Citigroup was estimated by CBO at $9 billion. Any losses to be incurred by the government would be reported above the line.
Support to GMAC	13	Capital support to GMAC under the Automotive Industry Financing Program.	13	See the reporting description for the CPP. The subsidy component of the assistance to the automotive industry was estimated by CBO at 73 percent. Any losses to be incurred by the government would be reported above the line.
2. Others				
Support to Fannie Mae and Freddie Mac	400	Up to $200 billion of equity injection for each government-sponsored enterprise (GSE).	400	The equity injections are reported as spending by the OMB and Treasury. The CBO reports as spending the subsidy cost (in present value terms adjusted for market risk) of the GSE takeovers.
Subtotal	741			

Table A2.3 (continued)

Program	Amount (billion)	Operations	Gross Treasury Financing Need	Reporting
Grants and purchase of assets and lending by Treasury				
I. TARP				
Home Affordable Modification Program	50	As part of the Homeowner Affordability and Stability Plan, the TARP would make direct payments to mortgage servicers to help homeowners refinance their mortgages. As of mid-June 2009, the Treasury had determined the recipients of about $15 billion, but no money had been disbursed.	50	The net cost of the program will be the full amount of payments made by the government.
Automotive Industry Financial Program	67	Loans to GM and Chrysler.	67	The CBO estimated the subsidy component of the assistance to the automotive industry at 73 percent. Any losses to be incurred by the government would be reported above the line.
Auto Supplier Support Program	5	Providing suppliers with access to government-backed protection for their receivables.	5	The CBO estimated the subsidy component of the assistance to the automotive industry at 73 percent. Any losses to be incurred by the government would be reported above the line.
Unlocking Credit for Small Business	15	The Treasury announced that it will be purchasing up to $15 billion in securities to boost the credit markets for small businesses.	15	
2. Others				
Credit Union Homeowners Affordability Relief Program and Credit Union System Investment Program	41	Two loan programs operate through the National Credit Union Administration's Central Liquidity Facility. The Credit Union Homeowners Affordability Relief Program is providing subsidized funding intended to help credit unions modify mortgages. The Credit Union System Investment Program seeks to facilitate lending by shoring up corporate credit unions.	0	
Subtotal	178			
Central bank liquidity support backed by Treasury				
I. TARP				
Term Asset-Backed Securities Loan Facility (TALF)	20	The Treasury made an initial pledge of $20 billion in TARP funding to cover the potential losses under the TALF. Proposed modifications to expand the program could involve additional commitments.	20	
2. Others				
Commercial Paper Funding Facility	50	The Treasury made a special deposit at the Federal Reserve Bank of New York in support of this facility.	50	The $50 billion are reported as a deposit with the Federal Reserve. Any losses resulting from calls on these guarantees will be reported by the government as spending (transfers).
Subtotal	70			
Liquidity provision and other support by central bank				
Maiden Lane II and III facilities and loan (AIG)	113	The Federal Reserve Board, with full support of the Treasury Department, authorized the New York Federal Reserve to lend to AIG. These comprise $53 billion in funding for purchases of distressed assets under Maiden Lane II and Maiden Lane III facilities, and a $60 billion loan.	0	

Maiden Lane I	26	The Federal Reserve authorized the New York Federal Reserve to provide nonrecourse lending to JP Morgan against assets of Bear Stearns under the Maiden Lane I facility.	0
Citigroup and Bank of America Support	321	The Treasury and FDIC will guarantee losses on troubled assets (over $300 billion). Total is $269 billion. $25 billion is from TARP ($20 billion for recap and $5 billion for guarantee), $10 billion is for guarantee by FDIC. The remaining amount ($234 billion) is from the Federal Reserve as lending. $87 billion support for Bank of America is also announced by the Federal Reserve.	0
Term Securities Lending Facility (TSLF)	75	Lending Treasuries against Treasuries, agencies, agency MBS, and all investment-grade securities. Volume at end-June 2009 was about $7 billion.	0
Term Auction Facility (TAF)	500	Lending funds at auctioned rate against discount window collateral. Volume at end-June 2009 was about $280 billion.	0
Commercial Paper Fund Facility (CPFF)	1,750	Purchasing highly rated 3-month unsecured and asset-backed commercial paper. The maximum commitment is $1.8 trillion. The Treasury has deposited $50 billion into an account at the New York Federal Reserve to support this facility. Volume at end-June 2009 was about $115 billion.	0
Money Market Investor Funding Facility (MMIFF)	540	Purchasing certificates of deposit and commercial paper issued by highly rated financial institutions. No purchases as of end-June 2009. Will expire on October 30, 2009.	0
Asset-Backed Commercial Paper Money Market Mutual Fund Liquidity Facility (AMLF)	15	Lending funds (nonrecourse) to a wide range of counterparties against highly rated first tier Asset-Backed Commercial Paper. Volume at end-June 2009 was about $15 billion.	0
Primary Dealer Credit Facility	0	Lending funds against a full range of tri-party repo system collateral. No lending as of end-June 2009.	0
TALF	180	Lending (nonrecourse) against newly issued ABS. Loans of up to 3 years, underlying securities may be of longer maturity. Volume at end-June 2009 was about $25 billion.	0
Subtotal	3,520		
Guarantees			
I. TARP			
Citigroup Asset Guarantee	5	Second-loss after the bank, with Treasury covering up to $5 billion and the Federal Deposit Insurance Corporation (FDIC) up to $10 billion.	5
Bank of America Asset Guarantee	8	For the second-loss after the bank on $10 billion, the Treasury (through TARP) and FDIC split the government's 90 percent share with the Treasury covering up to $7.5 billion and FDIC covering up to $2.5 billion. On June 25, 2009, Federal Open Market Committee (FOMC) Chairman Bernanke observed that the arrangement has not been consummated, also noting that Bank of America believes that protection is not needed.	8

The fees are reported as revenue in the government accounts. Costs resulting from calls on this guarantee will be reported as spending.

Table A2.3 (concluded)

Program	Amount (billion)	Operations	Gross Treasury Financing Need	Reporting
2. Others				
Citigroup Asset Guarantee	10	Second-loss after the bank, with Treasury covering up to $5 billion and the FDIC up to $10 billion.	0	
Temporary Guarantee Program for Money Market Funds	50	The Treasury guarantees (through September 18, 2009) participating investors that they will receive $1 for each money market fund share held as of close of business on September 19, 2008. The assets of the Exchange Stabilization Fund will be made available to guarantee payments as needed (up to $50 billion).	0	The fees are reported as revenue in the government accounts. Costs resulting from calls on this guarantee will be reported as spending.
Temporary Liquidity Guarantee Program	1,485	This program provides full guarantees for certain checking and other non-interest-bearing deposit accounts (Transaction Account Guarantee) and certain newly issued senior unsecured debt (Debt Guarantee). At end-May 2009, the amount of FDIC-guaranteed debt that can be issued by eligible entities was $785 billion (actual amounts outstanding were $346 billion). The amount covered by the transaction account guarantee was estimated at $700 billion.	0	The fees will be reported as revenue in the government accounts. Costs resulting from calls on this guarantee will be reported as spending.
Hope for Homeowners Program	1	This program permits home mortgages to be refinanced through private lenders with a guarantee from the FHA.	0	Expected to be reported by the FDIC as contingent liabilities.
Subtotal	*1,559*			
Total	6,067		960	
TARP total	510			

Appendix III Outlook for Recovery Rates

This appendix provides estimates of recovery rates for banking crises, and investigates their determinants to assess the outlook for recovery following the current crisis. The recovery rate is here defined as the proceeds recovered from the sale of assets in percent of the gross fiscal cost.

Magnitude of Recovery Rates

The key source of the recovery rate data is the Laeven and Valencia (2008) database. The recovery rate in this database is defined as the amount recovered during years t to $t+5$, where t denotes the start of the crisis, in percent of the gross budgetary outlays associated with the banking crisis. The following adjustments are made to the Laeven and Valencia (2008) database: (1) the gross fiscal cost of the Japan 1997 crisis is lowered from 14 percent of GDP to 9.1 percent of GDP (see Box A3.1); (2) the recovery amount associated with the Japan 1997 crisis is raised to 4.8 percent of GDP from

less than 0.1 percent of GDP (Box A3.1); and (3) the recovery amount associated with the U.S. crisis of 1988 (not included in the Laeven and Valencia database) is recorded as 1.6 percent of GDP based on Hoelscher and Quintyn (2003).

The recovery rate data have a wide range. For the 39 crises during 1980–2003 for which data are available, the recovery rates have a mean of 20 percent, a median of 8 percent, a maximum of 94 percent (Sweden, 1991), and minimum of zero (Figure A3.1). The net fiscal cost of budgetary outlays associated with the banking crises (gross cost minus recovery amounts) averaged 13 percent of GDP, with a median of 10 percent and a maximum of 55 percent of GDP (Argentina, 1980) (Figure A3.2).

What Determines the Recovery Rate?

We investigate the association between the recovery rate and the following variables: (1) the level of

---

Box A3.1. Japan's 1997 Banking Crisis: Fiscal Cost and Recovery Rates

Data from the Japan Deposit Insurance Corporation (JDIC) suggest that the fiscal cost of Japan's banking crisis was smaller, and the recovery rate higher than reported in existing studies. In particular, the data provide the following insights:

Total authorized amount. The amount of budget authorizations for measures related to the banking crisis totaled ¥70 trillion during 1997–2001, that is, 13.6 percent of GDP. Of the total amount, the bulk (¥57 trillion) corresponds to government guarantees to the JDIC, and the remainder (¥13 trillion) to government bond issuance to provide resources for grants to the financial institutions.

Gross fiscal cost. The JDIC data indicate that only 9.1 percent of GDP of the authorized amount was actually spent. This number is substantially lower than the fiscal cost reported in Laeven and Valencia (2008)

(14 percent of GDP), and in *The Economist* (2008) (24 percent of GDP).

Recovery rate and net fiscal cost. The cumulative amount of recoveries during 1997–2008 reached 4.8 percent of GDP, that is, 53 percent of the gross fiscal cost. If grants—that are unrecoverable by definition—are excluded from the gross cost, the recovery rate rises to 88 percent. These recovery rates are substantially larger than the rate recorded in the Laeven and Valencia (2008) database (less than 1 percent), which was based on recoveries collected during the first five years following the start of the crisis (1997–2002). This result suggests that it may take more than five years for substantial recovery amounts to accrue. In addition, some assets purchased from failed financial institutions—such as securities and real estate property—were eventually sold by the authorities at a gain, resulting in recovery rates in excess of 100 percent.

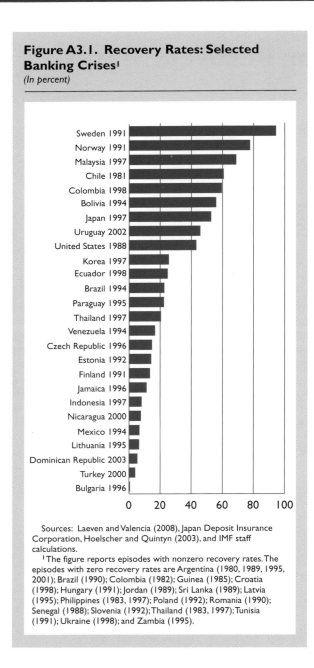

Figure A3.1. Recovery Rates: Selected Banking Crises[1]
(In percent)

Sources: Laeven and Valencia (2008), Japan Deposit Insurance Corporation, Hoelscher and Quintyn (2003), and IMF staff calculations.
[1] The figure reports episodes with nonzero recovery rates. The episodes with zero recovery rates are Argentina (1980, 1989, 1995, 2001); Brazil (1990); Colombia (1982); Guinea (1985); Croatia (1998); Hungary (1991); Jordan (1989); Sri Lanka (1989); Latvia (1995); Philippines (1983, 1997); Poland (1992); Romania (1990); Senegal (1988); Slovenia (1992); Thailand (1983, 1997); Tunisia (1991); Ukraine (1998); and Zambia (1995).

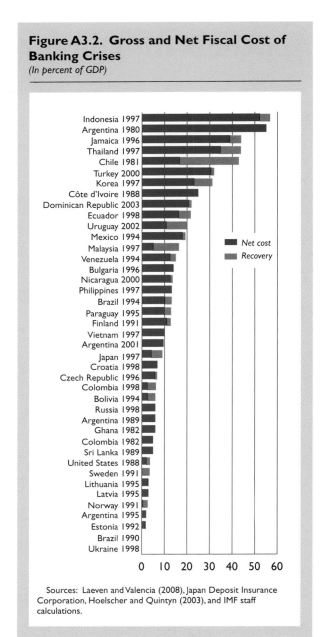

Figure A3.2. Gross and Net Fiscal Cost of Banking Crises
(In percent of GDP)

Sources: Laeven and Valencia (2008), Japan Deposit Insurance Corporation, Hoelscher and Quintyn (2003), and IMF staff calculations.

economic development (captured by per capita real PPP GDP); (2) a transition-country dummy;[41] (3) the occurrence of an exchange rate (ER) crisis (an ER crisis dummy that equals 1 when the nominal depreciation is in the top quintile of the full sample); (4) the gross fiscal cost of the crisis; and (5) "fiscal space" at the start of the banking crisis (measured by the fiscal balance/GDP ratio).

The regression results indicate a number of significant correlates of the recovery rate. The positive and significant correlation with per capita income suggests that advanced countries have higher recovery rates. Similarly, a transition country dummy has a significant and negative sign, suggesting that the nature of the losses arising in financial crises in transition countries implied lower recovery rates. Exchange rate crises are associated with lower recovery rates. This could be because in exchange rate crises, the initial

---

[41] Transition countries are as defined in IMF (2000).

Table A3.1. Estimation Results[1]
(Dependent variable: recovery rate)

	(1)	(2)	(3)	(4)	(5)	(6)	(7)
Log(PPP real GDP per capita)	15.18** [2.576]			14.54** [2.505]	13.91** [2.626]	12.96** [2.115]	11.27* [1.936]
Transition country dummy		−18.99*** [−3.152]		−18.25*** [−2.976]	−21.95*** [−2.826]	−17.29*** [−2.770]	−21.75*** [−2.774]
ER crisis dummy			−25.20*** [−5.245]	−19.80** [−2.677]	−20.11*** [−3.041]	−14.65* [−1.971]	−13.19* [−1.815]
Gross fiscal cost/GDP					−30.2 [−1.233]		−34.18 [−1.667]
Fiscal balance/GDP						195.2** [2.519]	215.4** [2.554]
Observations	38	38	38	38	38	37	37
Adjusted R-squared	0.15	0.06	0.12	0.31	0.32	0.37	0.39

Source: IMF staff estimates.

[1]The table reports *t*-statistics adjusted for clustering in parentheses. ***, **, * denote statistical significance at 1, 5, and 10 percent level, respectively.

outlays arise from the acquisition of liabilities that are inflated by sizable and permanent depreciations, as well as high interest rates, while the decline in the value of assets plays a less significant role. Recovery rates are higher, the larger the fiscal balance at the start of the crisis: countries entering a banking crisis with a larger "buffer stock" experienced less severe losses. This finding is consistent with the notion that a stronger fiscal position is associated with high-quality public financial management that improves the prospect for a recovery.[42] Recovery rates are also lower, the higher the gross fiscal cost of the crisis, although the relationship is not statistically significant. Table A3.1 reports the estimation results.

The estimated equation can also be used to project recovery rates. For the purposes of projecting recovery rates, the equation containing the full set of controls considered is used (column 7 in Table A3.1). The in-sample fit of this equation can be assessed based on the adjusted R^2 of 39 percent, and a mean absolute residual of 15 percentage points (Table A3.2). Out-of-sample predictions based on this estimated equation imply recovery rates for the current financial crisis averaging 47 percent, with an average 95 percent confidence interval of 28 to 68 percent. Based on these recovery rates, and current estimates of the gross fiscal cost of the crisis that average 3.6 percent of GDP for G-20 countries, the expected average net fiscal cost is 1.6 percent of GDP, with a 95 percent confidence interval of 0.9 to 2.2 percent of GDP (Table A2.1).

However, there are several caveats in using the historical estimated coefficients to project recovery rates: (1) this is the first crisis since the Great Depression where both the output decline and financial sector turmoil are global; (2) with many countries attempting the liquidation of assets over the coming years, recovery ratio could be lower; (3) the sample size is small (37 countries); and (4) there are only five advanced economies.

---

[42]Countries with stronger public financial management systems could be countries that adopted better processes for managing and selling the assets acquired through financial support operations. Further work would be needed to measure, and use as regressor, a variable capturing directly differences in those processes across countries.

Table A3.2. In-Sample Recovery Rate Predictions[1]

(In percent)

	Year	Prediction	Actual	Residual
Argentina	1980	6.9	0.0	−6.9
Argentina	1989	1.3	0.0	−1.3
Argentina	1995	40.2	0.0	−40.2
Argentina	2001	16.4	0.0	−16.4
Bolivia	1994	21.7	56.0	34.3
Brazil	1990	30.1	0.0	−30.1
Brazil	1994	29.8	22.7	−7.1
Chile	1981	30.6	60.8	30.3
Colombia	1982	11.1	0.0	−11.1
Colombia	1998	29.1	59.6	30.4
Croatia	1998	11.7	0.0	−11.7
Czech Republic	1996	22.9	14.7	−8.2
Dominican Republic	2003	16.2	5.5	−10.7
Ecuador	1998	16.4	24.9	8.5
Estonia	1992	18.4	14.2	−4.2
Finland	1991	47.5	13.4	−34.1
Guinea	1985	21.3	0.0	−21.3
Hungary	1991	10.2	0.0	−10.2
Indonesia	1997	13.3	8.1	−5.2
Jamaica	1996	10.5	11.3	0.8
Japan	1997	43.8	52.7	9.0
Jordan	1989	14.5	0.0	−14.5
Korea	1997	36.2	25.6	−10.6
Latvia	1995	9.8	0.0	−9.8
Lithuania	1995	8.3	6.5	−1.8
Malaysia	1997	47.8	68.9	21.1
Mexico	1994	28.2	6.7	−21.5
Nicaragua	2000	16.8	7.6	−9.2
Norway	1991	53.2	77.8	24.6
Paraguay	1995	35.7	22.5	−13.3
Philippines	1983	27.6	0.0	−27.6
Philippines	1997	26.1	0.0	−26.1
Poland	1992	2.9	0.0	−2.9
Romania	1990	4.3	0.0	−4.3
Senegal	1988	15.4	0.0	−15.4
Slovenia	1992	24.5	0.0	−24.5
Sri Lanka	1989	9.9	0.0	−9.9
Sweden	1991	52.1	94.4	42.4
Thailand	1983	21.6	0.0	−21.6
Thailand	1997	22.4	20.5	−1.9
Tunisia	1991	23.9	0.0	−23.9
Turkey	2000	12.8	4.1	−8.8
Ukraine	1998	8.6	0.0	−8.6
United States	1988	47.2	43.2	−3.9
Uruguay	2002	25.2	45.8	20.7
Venezuela	1994	12.5	16.7	4.2
Zambia	1995	8.6	0.0	−8.6
Memorandum item:				
Mean absolute residual				15.2

Source: IMF staff estimates.

[1]The table reports in-sample prediction based on equation 7 (full set of controls), and predictions for gross fiscal cost.

Appendix IV Measuring Government Contingent Liabilities to the Banking Sector

This appendix provides illustrative estimates of the fiscal cost of government contingent liabilities related to banking sector implicit and explicit guarantees. The eventual cost of these guarantees is subject to significant uncertainty and will depend on the evolution of the financial sector and of the economy. Thus, we provide here a range of estimates broadly based on the contingent claims approach (CCA), derived from modern finance theory.[43]

The main idea behind this approach is to combine balance sheet information of financial institutions with measures of risk that institutions may face. Intuitively, the potential cost for the government arising from guarantees depends on the probability that the value of banks' assets falls below the value of the banks' liabilities (including deposits, interbank loans, etc.), and by the extent of the imbalance. In turn, these depend on the structure of bank assets and liabilities, on the market value of the latter, and on the volatility in these values. For example, an increase in volatility will raise the probability that, as a result of market movements, a bank's net worth becomes negative.

To implement CCA, standard option-pricing theory is utilized. The option-pricing formulas applied in CCA to estimate the banks' credit risk and their expected losses rely on a few selected variables including the asset value, volatility of the asset return, risk-free value of debt, the time horizon until the expiration date of the guarantee, and the risk-free interest rate (Black and Scholes, 1973; and Merton, 1973). The guarantee can be modeled as a *put option*[44] on the asset with an exercise price equal to the face value of debt—an option sold by the guarantor (the government). In effect, the guarantee gives the bank the right to "sell" the assets to the guarantor in exchange for a payment equal to the face value of the debt. As with any put option, the bank would exercise the option only if the value of the assets falls below the face value of the debt—that is, in case of default. The CCA computes the value of these put options assuming that all debt and deposits are guaranteed—through explicit or implicit guarantees.

Operationally, we utilize a methodology developed by Moody's in conjunction with others (hereafter MKMV). Specifically, the potential expected loss to governments is the implicit put option values as obtained from MKMV's credit risk spread measure—known as the expected default frequency implied credit default swap (EICDS). EICDS combines a probability of default by a bank on its debt obligations—called the expected default frequency (EDF) with the likely recovery on assets acquired by the government; the latter is measured by the so-called loss given default (LGD). The LGD is calibrated in such a way that the EICDS measure matches closely the observed market CDSs.

The expected losses for governments from guarantees on banks are estimated for two groups of countries: (1) G-7 and advanced non-G-7 countries (Australia, Austria, Belgium, Denmark, Ireland, Korea, Netherlands, Norway, Portugal, Spain, Sweden, and Switzerland); and (2) emerging markets (Greece, Hungary, Russia, and Saudi Arabia).[45]

The present discounted value of expected losses associated with guarantees over a five-year horizon and under three recovery scenarios were computed. The losses were calculated using the MKMV contingent claims model.[46] Given the sensitivity of the results to the assumed recovery rates on assets, three scenarios were considered: (1) the base case (using MKMV estimated recovery rates); (2) a conservative recovery rate (of 40 percent for all banks—frequently assumed in many CDS models); and (3) an optimistic scenario (80 percent recovery rate).

The results suggest substantial potential pressure on the countries' fiscal positions. Under the first scenario (column A, Table A4.1) governments' losses over five years are projected to be the largest in relation to GDP

---

[43]See Gray, Merton, and Bodie (2007 and 2008) and Gray and Malone (2008) for further details about the CCA methodology.

[44]A put option is the right to sell the underlying asset at a specified exercise price by a certain expiration date.

[45]The country classification of emerging markets is different than the one that is traditionally used in the IMF. In particular, Greece is classified as an advanced economy by the IMF. The countries that are included in the emerging market economies in this work are not very representative of this group.

[46]MKMV calculates the CCA models and expected losses for banks with traded equity and those without traded equity are not in the database.

Table A4.1. Banking Sector: Expected Cost of Financial Guarantees Based on CCA Calculations[1]
(In percent of GDP)

	Total Implicit Put Value		
	MKMV LGD[2] (A)	Conservative LGD[2] (B)	Optimistic LGD[2] (C)
Advanced economies[3]	14.4	28.1	9.4
Emerging market economies[4]	4.1	4.5	1.5
Total	13.6	26.3	8.8

Sources: Moody's KMV CreditEdge; and IMF staff estimates.

[1]Assuming full guarantees to all banks (systemic and small). Numbers are weighted by PPP GDP of 2007.

[2]MKMV LGD, conservative LGD, and optimistic LGD refer, respectively, to (1) Moody's estimated recovery rates (equivalently 1 − loss given default (LGD)), (2) a conservative recovery rate of 40 percent, and (3) an optimistic recovery rate of 80 percent.

[3]Advanced economies include our sample of G-7 and non-G-7 advanced economies (Australia, Austria, Belgium, Denmark, Ireland, Korea, Netherlands, Norway, Portugal, Spain, Sweden, and Switzerland).

[4]Emerging market economies: Greece, Hungary, Russia, and Saudi Arabia.

in the advanced economies (14½ percent of GDP). These are over three times larger than for the emerging market group. Even under optimistic assumptions (column C), in the advanced economies, losses would amount to over 9 percent of GDP. Assuming lower recovery rates increases the size of the expected losses very significantly (column B).

The fraction of the expected losses that would likely be covered by government guarantees varies across countries. The fraction would depend on whether small nonsystemically important banks are allowed to fail or some debt holders end up not benefiting from a full guarantee in the event of default. Given that the size of expected losses increases with that of the banks, it is often the case that only large banks benefit from government guarantees or that the government guarantees are a combination of a blanket guarantee of all deposits (deposits are typically 40 to 60 percent of bank liabilities) up to a certain amount and a partial guarantee of banks' other liabilities. Therefore, in most instances *contingent fiscal liabilities* would likely represent a fraction of the *expected losses* presented above. A rough proxy for such fraction could be the proportion of losses that is accounted for by the largest banks. Table A4.2 assumes that the government guarantees 75 percent of the estimated expected losses reported in Table A4.1 above, and reports the annual fiscal cost (i.e., the losses spread equally over the five years).

The reported results may overstate governments' costs owing to the increase in market risk premia over the recent period. Estimating the fiscal costs of bank liabilities and the explicit financial support is a dynamic process: these could be large in the early stages or during a crisis, but are likely to fall after a restructuring process has taken place.

The analysis could be complemented in several ways. The estimates presented above provide a good indication of the range of contingent liabilities for governments associated with banks' liabilities, but they do not take into account potential future equity injections or other forms of support for the banking system. Large equity injections may reduce the losses on debt and deposits, increase recovery rates, and thus reduce the cost of the guarantees.

As a complementary measure to the MKMV estimate, we also calculate the potential cost to the government of providing guarantees by an alternative approach. This approach simply entails multiplying the EICDS by the total of banks' liabilities that are guaranteed. The EICDS spread can in effect be regarded as being indicative of the insurance premium on banks' liabilities and provides a simple way to estimate the costs to the government of providing this "insurance." We should note, however, that an EICDS spread (based on market information) in the presence of government guarantees of liabilities may not fully capture government's risk and thus multiplying it by the liabilities may entail a downward bias in the potential cost to the government. A range of CDS spreads are therefore calculated to assess the possible bias. In particular, the "conservative" CDS spread based on estimates of the present value of expected losses and multiplied by the amount of liabilities should be seen as an upper bound of the potential cost to the government. This approach is applied to compute the cost of the explicit guarantees provided by governments as discussed in the main paper (Section II). Aside from the cost of these explicit guarantees, it could be argued that there are also implicit guarantees stemming from too-big-to-fail or too-systemic-to-fail considerations. Thus, we report below the estimated cost of an implicit guarantee on the total of banking sector liabilities.

Table A4.2. Banking Sector: Expected Cost of Financial Guarantees Based on CCA Calculations Annual Cost Over Five Years[1]
(In percent of GDP)

	Total Implicit Put Value		
	MKMV LGD[2] (A)	Conservative LGD[2] (B)	Optimistic LGD[2] (C)
Advanced economies[3]	2.2	4.2	1.4
Emerging market economies[4]	0.6	0.7	0.2
Total	2.0	3.9	1.3

Sources: Moody's KMV CreditEdge; and IMF staff estimates.

[1]Assuming that 75 percent of the total expected losses for all the banks represents the contingent liability of the government. This is an annual cost figure over five years. Numbers are weighted by PPP GDP of 2007.

[2]MKMV LGD, conservative LGD, and optimistic LGD refer, respectively, to (1) Moody's estimated recovery rates (equivalently 1 − loss given default (LGD)), (2) a conservative recovery rate of 40 percent, and (3) an optimistic recovery rate of 80 percent.

[3]Advanced economies include our sample of G-7 and non-G-7 advanced economies (Australia, Austria, Belgium, Denmark, Ireland, Korea, Netherlands, Norway, Portugal, Spain, Sweden, and Switzerland).

[4]Emerging market economies: Greece, Hungary, Russia, and Saudi Arabia.

Table A4.3. Banking Sector: Expected Costs of Financial Guarantees Based on Three Alternative Credit Spread Measures and Total Banking Liabilities[1]
(In percent of GDP)

	Expected Costs Based on		
	MKMV CDS-A[2,3] (A)	Conservative case CDS-B[2,3] (B)	Optimistic case CDS-C[2,3] (C)
Total[4]	4.0	8.4	2.5
Advanced economies	4.3	9.0	2.7
Emerging market economies	1.7	2.0	0.6

Sources: Moody's KMV CreditEdge; and IMF staff estimates.

[1]Assuming full guarantees to all banks.

[2]Spreads are calculated based on estimates of implicit put option values for individual banks and using Moody's KMV CreditEdge database as of November 14, 2008. They are based on a five-year average duration.

[3]MKMV LGD, conservative LGD, and optimistic LGD refer, respectively, to (1) Moody's estimated recovery rates (equivalently 1 − loss given default (LGD)), (2) a conservative recovery rate of 40 percent, and (3) an optimistic recovery rate of 80 percent.

[4]Numbers are weighted by PPP GDP of 2007.

The results using the complementary approach are substantially larger than those obtained above. CDS spreads are calculated based on estimates of the present value of expected losses in the three scenarios noted earlier (Table A4.3): MKMV (column A), conservative (column B), and optimistic (column C). The results show that the annual expected costs under the conservative scenario are significantly larger than the costs under the base case scenario.

Appendix V   Estimation of Nondiscretionary Impacts

Methodology for Calculating the Estimated Impact of Automatic Stabilizers

The impact on fiscal balances from automatic stabilizers was computed as the change in the cyclical balance between two consecutive years. The cyclical balance in year t was estimated as the difference between the overall balance in percent of GDP (OB_t) and the cyclically adjusted balance in percent of potential GDP ($CAOB_t$), which was computed as

$$CAOB_t = OB_t - (\eta_{Rt} - \eta_{Gt}) * GAP_t,$$

where GAP_t is the output gap, calculated as the ratio of output to potential GDP minus one.[47] Output gap estimates were taken from the IMF's April 2009 *World Economic Outlook Update* for all G-20 countries, except Indonesia and Saudi Arabia. For these two countries, potential GDP was computed as trend-GDP using a Hodrick-Prescott filter with the smoothing parameter 6.25.[48] η_{Rt} and η_{Gt} are revenue and expenditure budgetary-sensitivity parameters defined as

$$\eta_{Rt} = (\varepsilon_R - 1)\frac{R_t}{Y_t} \text{ and } \eta_{Gt} = (\varepsilon_G - 1)\frac{G_t}{Y_t},$$

where ε_R and ε_G are revenue and expenditure elasticities with respect to the output gap assumed to be constant over time and R_t/Y_t and G_t/Y_t are ratios of primary revenue and expenditure to GDP.

Hence, the contribution from automatic stabilizers is, effectively, the first difference (change between the two consecutive years) of the output gap multiplied by the difference of revenue and expenditure budgetary-sensitivity parameters, namely:

$$AS_t = \Delta COB_t = \Delta[(\eta_{Rt} - \eta_{Gt}) * GAP_t].$$

The estimates of revenue and expenditure elasticities were obtained as follows. Girouard and André (2005) provide estimates for ε_R and ε_G for a number of advanced countries. For other G-20 countries, revenue elasticity ε_R was assumed to be equal to 1, and expenditure elasticity ε_G was set equal to zero. In this simple case, the contribution from automatic stabilizers becomes

$$AS_t = \Delta\left[\frac{G_t}{Y_t} * GAP_t\right].$$

With no significant change in government size between two consecutive years, the contribution from automatic stabilizers can be further approximated by

$$AS_t \approx \frac{G_t}{Y_t}\Delta GAP_t.$$

Estimates of the impact of the automatic stabilizers on G-20 fiscal balances in 2008 and 2009 using this approach are shown in Table A5.1.[49]

Estimates of the Impact of Other Nondiscretionary Factors

As noted in the main paper, looking just at the influence of output gap changes is not sufficient to evaluate the effect of nondiscretionary factors on budgetary positions. This is because some variables affecting fiscal balances are not perfectly correlated with output fluctuations. For example, exceptional declines in asset prices—that is, significantly above or below what

---

[47]The use of total GDP has limitations for commodity-producing countries, given different cycles. However, due to limited data on non-oil GDP, the paper uses overall GDP for the estimates.

[48]The estimates extend the growth projections of the *World Economic Outlook*, April 2009 through the year 2020 for the calculation of trend output.

[49]Estimates of the impact of automatic stabilizers based on other approaches such as use of more detailed information about the behavior of revenue and spending in specific countries and calculation of stabilizers as the difference between the overall and structural balances may yield somewhat different results.

Table A5.1. Estimated Impact of Automatic Stabilizers on G-20 Fiscal Balances
(In percent of GDP, relative to the previous year)

	2008	2009
United States	−0.4	−1.7
China	−0.1	−0.6
Japan	−0.6	−2.6
India	0.0	−0.6
Germany	0.0	−3.5
Russia	0.7	−2.8
United Kingdom	−0.4	−2.4
France	−0.5	−2.4
Brazil	0.6	−1.8
Italy	−0.8	−2.7
Mexico	−0.4	−1.5
Spain	−0.7	−1.8
Canada	−0.7	−1.8
Korea	−0.1	−1.7
Turkey	−0.7	−2.4
Indonesia	0.2	−0.4
Australia	−0.4	−1.2
Saudi Arabia	0.4	−1.3
Argentina	0.1	−1.5
South Africa	−0.2	−1.1
PPP-weighted average	−0.2	−1.8

Sources: IMF, *World Economic Outlook*, April 2009; and IMF staff estimates.

Estimation

To assess the cost for fiscal revenues of equity and housing market price declines, staff regressions from a sample of advanced and emerging market countries were used to derive parameters that could be applied across the sample. Country-specific parameters would have been preferable, given country-by-country differences in, for example, financial markets and taxation (see Morris and Schuknecht, 2007). However, a simpler approach was followed, in light of time and data constraints, as well as the aim of deriving estimates of broadly comparable and illustrative costs. This involved estimating regressions of the form:

$$\Delta CAR_t = F + \beta^t \Delta\%E_t + \beta^{t-1}\Delta\%E_{t-1} + \lambda^t\Delta\%H_t + \lambda^{t-1}\Delta\%H_{t-1},$$

where ΔCAR_t is the first difference in cyclically adjusted revenue as a share of potential GDP; F are country-specific fixed effects; E_t and H_t are, respectively, real equity and real housing prices.[50]

---

[50]Cyclically adjusted revenue data are based on the April 2009 *World Economic Outlook*, using the methodology described in the section "Methodology for Calculating the Estimated Impact of Automatic Stabilizers." Housing price data and projections through 2009 covering 10 countries are from the IMF's Research Department; data for some other G-20 countries (Brazil, India, Indonesia, Russia, and South Africa) were obtained from international real estate and investment banking sources. Equity price data are from Bloomberg, with GDP deflators from the IMF's *World Economic Outlook* used to convert nominal prices to real terms; data were obtained starting from 1990, with annual growth indicators from 1991.

might be considered "normal" levels—may reduce revenues by more than could be explained just by looking at output gap changes.

Table A5.2. Responsiveness of Cyclically Adjusted Revenue to Asset Price Changes[1]

	10 Countries, 1991–2007							20 Countries, 1991–2007		
	(1)	(2)	(3)	(4)	(5)	(6)	(7)	(8)	(9)	(10)
Real house prices	...	−1.67	−0.62	...	−1.43	−0.14	...	...	...	...
(Std. error)	...	(1.47)	(1.24)	...	(1.58)	(1.33)	...	...	...	...
P-value (in percent)	...	25.8	61.5	...	36.7	91.7	...	...	...	...
Real house prices (lag)	2.69	1.79	...	0.95	3.36	...	2.07	...	...	...
(Std. error)	(1.38)	(1.37)	...	(1.15)	(1.57)	...	(1.36)	...	...	...
P-value (in percent)	5.3	19.3	...	41.2	3.4	...	13.1	...	...	...
Real equity prices	0.67	...	...	...	0.66	0.63	...	0.52	0.04	...
(Std. error)	(0.32)	...	...	...	(0.32)	(0.32)	...	(0.26)	(0.22)	...
P-value (in percent)	3.8	...	...	...	4.2	4.9	...	4.8	86.2	...
Real equity prices (lag)	0.79	...	...	...	0.79	...	0.82	0.94	...	0.83
(Std. error)	(0.32)	...	...	...	(0.32)	...	(0.32)	(0.23)	...	(0.22)
P-value (in percent)	1.4	...	...	...	1.3	...	1.2	0.0	...	0.0
R-squared	0.17	0.07	0.06	0.07	0.17	0.09	0.14	0.15	0.09	0.14

Sources: IMF, *World Economic Outlook*; Bloomberg; international real estate and investment banking sources; and IMF staff estimates.

[1]Explanatory variables are percent change in corresponding asset price for end-of-period values. Dependent variable is the first difference of cyclically adjusted revenue as a share of potential GDP. Country fixed effects are included.

Results

The results are presented in Table A5.2. The estimated coefficients represent the percentage point change in cyclically adjusted revenue for a given real change in asset prices. The estimates from column 1 were used in the main paper. They suggest that a 10 percent decline in equity prices leads to a cyclically adjusted decline in revenues by 0.07 and 0.08 percent of GDP in the current and subsequent years. The 0.15 percent of GDP cumulative effect is close to estimates for selected countries in Europe in Morris and Schuknecht (2007). For housing, a 10 percent decline in prices leads to a 0.27 percent of GDP decline in cyclically adjusted revenues in the following year (the contemporaneous term was excluded).

As the dependent variable is *cyclically adjusted revenue*, staff estimates measure the impact of housing and equity price changes *beyond* the normal cycle. If these asset prices moved in the same fashion as the business cycle, then the coefficients should be zero, as the standard cyclical adjustment should capture this effect.

Appendix VI Fiscal Stimulus Packages in the G-20 Countries

This appendix provides a summary of the fiscal stimulus packages announced in late 2008 and in the first several months of 2009 in the G-20 countries. For each country, information is provided on the type of measure (expenditure or revenue), its nature (permanent, temporary, or self-reversing), and its estimated budgetary cost and time profile, where available (Table A6.1).[51] Data

are expressed in U.S. dollars (unless otherwise indicated) and reflect staff's assessment of the authorities' estimates. For example, support to financial institutions are typically included in national authorities' announced packages, but they have been excluded here if these operations are already covered in Appendix II of this paper. Similarly, announced measures that staff have been able to determine were not genuinely new and crisis related have also been excluded.

The data are derived from several sources, including government announcements, websites, and reports. As national authorities continue to take measures to stem the crisis, this appendix reflects the status and information available through mid-May 2009.

---

[51]*Temporary* measures have a temporary effect on the deficit but a permanent impact on the debt level (e.g., expenditure measures that are one-off or designed to expire after a certain period). *Permanent* measures have a permanent effect on the deficit, and a cumulative one on debt (e.g., most revenue measures seem permanent). *Self-reversing* measures have a temporary effect on both deficits and debts.

Table A6.1. Summary of the Fiscal Stimulus Packages in the G-20 Countries
(In billions of U.S. dollars, unless otherwise stated)

Measure	Nature	Cost 2009	2010
Argentina			
Expenditure		3.4	...
Infrastructure investment	Temporary	3.0	...
Support to small and medium-sized enterprises (SMEs) and/or farmers	...	...	...
Safety nets	Temporary	0.3	...
Housing/construction support	...	...	...
Strategic industries support	...	...	...
Increase in public wage bill	...	...	...
Other	...	...	...
Revenue		1.3	
Personal income tax (PIT)/exemptions/deductions	Permanent	0.7	...
Indirect tax reductions	Permanent	0.6	...
Corporate income tax (CIT)/depreciation/incentives	...	...	...
Other	...	...	...
Memorandum items:			
Total cost		4.7	...
In percent of GDP		1.5	...
Australia			
Expenditure		18.1	14.7
Infrastructure investment	Temporary	4.0	5.0
Support to SMEs and/or farmers	...	...	...
Safety nets	Temporary	8.3	3.3
Housing/construction support	Temporary	0.7	0.3
Strategic industries support	...	...	...
Increase in public wage bill	...	...	...
Other	Temporary	5.1	6.2

Table A6.1 *(continued)*

Measure	Nature	Cost 2009	Cost 2010
Revenue		1.0	1.2
PIT/exemptions/deductions	...	...	...
Indirect tax reductions	...	...	...
CIT/depreciation/incentives	Temporary	0.4	0.8
Other	Temporary	0.6	0.4
Memorandum items:			
Total cost		19.1	15.9
In percent of GDP		2.5	2.1
Brazil[1]			
Expenditure		2.9	6.3
Infrastructure investment	...	...	...
Support to SMEs and/or farmers	...	...	...
Safety nets	Temporary	0.2	...
Housing/construction support	Temporary	2.7	6.3
Strategic industries support	...	...	...
Increase in public wage bill	...	...	...
Other	Temporary	...	...
Revenue		4.9	0.9
PIT/exemptions/deductions	Temporary	2.4	0.6
Indirect tax reductions	Temporary	1.3	...
CIT/depreciation/incentives	Permanent	...	...
Other	...	1.2	0.3
Memorandum items:			
Total cost in 2009		7.8	7.1
In percent of GDP		0.6	0.5
Canada[1]			
Expenditure		19.6	15.0
Infrastructure investment	Temporary	11.2	8.4
Support to SMEs and/or farmers	Temporary	...	...
Safety nets	Temporary	2.9	3.5
Housing/construction support	Temporary	3.7	1.7
Strategic industries support	Temporary	...	...
Increase in public wage bill	...	...	...
Other	Temporary	1.9	1.4
Revenue		3.5	5.1
PIT/exemptions/deductions	Permanent	2.8	4.3
Indirect tax reductions	...	...	...
CIT/depreciation/incentives	Permanent	0.6	0.8
Other	...	...	...
Memorandum items:			
Total cost		23.1	20.9
In percent of GDP		1.9	1.7
China[1,2]			
Expenditure		149.8	...
Infrastructure investment	Temporary	115.4	...
Support to SMEs and/or farmers	...	...	...
Safety nets	Temporary	...	...
Housing/construction support	Temporary	15.0	...
Strategic industries support	Temporary	13.9	...
Increase in public wage bill	...	...	...
Other	Temporary	5.6	...
Revenue		...	...
PIT/exemptions/deductions	...	...	...
Indirect tax reductions	Permanent	...	...
CIT/depreciation/incentives	...	...	...
Other	...	...	...

Table A6.1 *(continued)*

Measure	Nature	Cost 2009	Cost 2010
Memorandum items:			
Total cost		149.8	143.2
In percent of GDP		3.1	2.7
France			
Expenditure		15.1	2.6
Infrastructure investment	Temporary	6.8	1.8
Support to SMEs and/or farmers	…	…	…
Safety nets	Temporary	3.0	…
Housing/construction support	Temporary	0.9	0.8
Strategic industries support	…	…	…
Increase in public wage bill	…	…	…
Other	Temporary	4.3	…
Revenue		1.4	18.8
PIT/exemptions/deductions	Temporary	1.4	0.1
Indirect tax reductions	Permanent	…	3.4
CIT/depreciation/incentives	…	…	15.3
Other	…	…	…
Memorandum items:			
Total cost		16.5	21.4
In percent of GDP		0.7	0.8
Germany[1]			
Expenditure		31.8	25.4
Infrastructure investment	Temporary	13.0	12.8
Support to SMEs and/or farmers	Temporary	0.6	1.8
Safety nets	Permanent	9.0	7.7
Housing/construction support	Permanent	…	…
Strategic industries support	Temporary	0.1	0.2
Increase in public wage bill	…	…	…
Other	Temporary	9.1	2.9
Revenue		16.0	34.6
PIT/exemptions/deductions	Permanent	12.8	27.9
Indirect tax reductions	Permanent	0.1	0.2
CIT/depreciation/incentives	Permanent	3.1	6.5
Other	…	…	…
Memorandum items:			
Total cost		47.7	60.0
In percent of GDP		1.6	2.0
India[3]			
Expenditure		…	…
Infrastructure investment	Temporary	…	…
Support to SMEs and/or farmers	…	…	…
Safety nets	Temporary	…	…
Housing/construction support	Temporary	…	…
Strategic industries support	…	…	…
Increase in public wage bill	…	…	…
Other	Temporary	…	…
Revenue		6.3	7.6
PIT/exemptions/deductions	…	…	…
Indirect tax reductions	Temporary	6.3	7.6
CIT/depreciation/incentives	…	…	…
Other	…	…	…
Memorandum items:			
Total cost		6.3	7.6
In percent of GDP		0.6	0.6

Table A6.1 *(continued)*

Measure	Nature	Cost 2009	Cost 2010
Indonesia			
Expenditure		1.5	...
Infrastructure investment	Temporary	1.0	...
Support to SMEs and/or farmers	...	...	...
Safety nets	Temporary	0.5	...
Housing/construction support	...	...	...
Strategic industries support	...	...	...
Increase in public wage bill	...	...	...
Other	Temporary	0.0	...
Revenue		4.9	3.3
PIT/exemptions/deductions	Permanent	2.7	0.6
Indirect tax reductions	Permanent	0.5	0.5
CIT/depreciation/incentives	Permanent	1.7	2.2
Other	...	...	...
Memorandum items:			
Total cost		6.4	3.3
In percent of GDP		1.4	0.6
Italy[4]			
Expenditure		3.4	0.7
Infrastructure investment	Temporary	0.4	0.5
Support to SMEs and/or farmers	...	...	...
Safety nets	Temporary	3.1	...
Housing/construction support	Temporary	0.5	...
Strategic industries support	Temporary	...	...
Increase in public wage bill	...	...	...
Other	Temporary	−0.6	0.3
Revenue		−0.3	1.2
PIT/exemptions/deductions	Temporary	1.7	1.1
Indirect tax reductions	Temporary	−0.6	0.1
CIT/depreciation/incentives	Permanent	0.3	0.8
Other	Permanent	−1.8	−0.8
Memorandum items:			
Total cost (net)		4.5	1.9
In percent of GDP		0.2	0.1
Japan			
Expenditure		113.6	80.1
Infrastructure investment	Temporary	15.9	27.5
Support to SMEs and/or farmers	Temporary	...	...
Safety nets	Temporary	47.3	9.8
Housing/construction support	Temporary	2.1	0.4
Strategic industries support	...	...	...
Increase in public wage bill	...	...	...
Other	Temporary	48.3	42.5
Revenue		7.2	5.0
PIT/exemptions/deductions	Permanent	2.1	1.4
Indirect tax reductions	...	...	...
CIT/depreciation/incentives	Permanent	2.6	1.8
Other	Permanent	2.5	1.8
Memorandum items:			
Total cost		120.8	85.1
In percent of GDP		2.4	1.8
Korea[1]			
Expenditure		19.4	...
Infrastructure investment	Temporary	7.2	...
Support to SMEs and/or farmers	Temporary	5.6	...
Safety nets	Temporary	6.6	...

Table A6.1 (continued)

Measure	Nature	Cost 2009	Cost 2010
Housing/construction support	Temporary	...	...
Strategic industries support	...	...	...
Increase in public wage bill	...	...	...
Other	Temporary	...	...
Revenue		7.3	9.2
PIT/exemptions/deductions	Permanent	1.9	2.5
Indirect tax reductions	Temporary	0.9	...
CIT/depreciation/incentives	Permanent	4.3	6.4
Other	Temporary	0.1	0.3
Memorandum items:			
Total cost		26.7	9.2
In percent of GDP		3.7	1.2
Mexico[1]			
Expenditure		9.9	...
Infrastructure investment	Temporary	4.7	...
Support to SMEs and/or farmers	...	...	...
Safety nets	Temporary	5.2	...
Housing/construction support	...	...	...
Strategic industries support	...	...	...
Increase in public wage bill	...	...	...
Other	Temporary	...	...
Revenue		...	...
PIT/exemptions/deductions	...	...	...
Indirect tax reductions	...	...	...
CIT/depreciation/incentives	...	...	...
Other	...	...	...
Memorandum items:			
Total cost		12.4	...
In percent of GDP		1.5	...
Russia			
Expenditure		32.9	1.1
Infrastructure investment	...	...	...
Support to SMEs and/or farmers	Temporary	1.0	...
Safety nets	Temporary	14.7	1.1
Housing/construction support	Temporary	2.4	...
Strategic industries support	Temporary	6.2	...
Increase in public wage bill	...	...	...
Other	Temporary	8.6	...
Revenue		14.6	16.7
PIT/exemptions/deductions	Permanent	1.2	1.4
Indirect tax reductions	...	...	...
CIT/depreciation/incentives	Permanent	11.9	13.6
Other	...	1.5	1.7
Memorandum items:			
Total cost		47.5	17.8
In percent of GDP		4.1	1.3
Saudi Arabia[1]			
Expenditure		...	...
Infrastructure investment	Temporary	...	...
Support to SMEs and/or farmers	...	...	...
Safety nets	...	...	...
Housing/construction support	...	...	...
Strategic industries support	...	...	...
Increase in public wage bill	...	...	...
Other	...	...	...

Table A6.1 *(continued)*

Measure	Nature	Cost 2009	Cost 2010
Revenue		...	...
PIT/exemptions/deductions	...	...	...
Indirect tax reductions	...	...	...
CIT/depreciation/incentives	...	...	...
Other	...	...	...
Memorandum items:			
Total cost		12.3	14.8
In percent of GDP		3.3	3.5
South Africa[5]			
Expenditure		7.3	5.2
Infrastructure investment	Temporary	4.3	2.8
Support to SMEs and/or farmers	...	...	...
Safety nets	Temporary	2.2	1.8
Housing/construction support	Temporary	0.7	0.6
Strategic industries support	...	...	...
Increase in public wage bill	...	...	...
Other	...	...	...
Revenue		...	...
PIT/exemptions/deductions	...	...	...
Indirect tax reductions	...	...	...
CIT/depreciation/incentives	...	...	...
Other	...	...	...
Memorandum items:			
Total cost		7.3	5.2
In percent of GDP		3.0	2.1
Spain[9]			
Expenditure		14.6	...
Infrastructure investment	Temporary	10.7	...
Support to SMEs and/or farmers	...	...	...
Safety nets	Temporary	0.8	...
Housing/construction support	Temporary	0.1	...
Strategic industries support	Temporary	2.3	...
Increase in public wage bill	...	...	...
Other	Temporary	0.8	...
Revenue		15.2	1.7
PIT/exemptions/deductions	Permanent	7.3	9.5
Indirect tax reductions	Self-reversing	7.9	−7.8
CIT/depreciation/incentives	...	...	...
Other	...	...	...
Memorandum items:			
Total cost		32.1	...
In percent of GDP		2.3	...
Turkey			
Expenditure		2.1	0.3
Infrastructure investment	...	...	...
Support to SMEs and/or farmers	Temporary	0.1	...
Safety nets	Temporary	0.8	0.1
Housing/construction support	...	...	...
Strategic industries support	Temporary	0.2	...
Increase in public wage bill	...	...	...
Other	Temporary	1.0	0.2
Revenue		2.2	1.2
PIT/exemptions/deductions	Permanent	0.0	0.0
Indirect tax reductions	Temporary	1.6	0.1
CIT/depreciation/incentives	Permanent	0.3	0.5
Other	Permanent	0.2	0.6

Table A6.1 (concluded)

Measure	Nature	Cost 2009	Cost 2010
Memorandum items:			
Total cost		4.3	1.5
In percent of GDP		0.8	0.3
United Kingdom[7]			
Expenditure		6.4	−6.7
Infrastructure investment	Self-reversing	2.8	−2.2
Support to SMEs and/or farmers	...	...	...
Safety nets	Temporary	1.7	1.2
Housing/construction support	Temporary	1.5	−0.4
Strategic industries support	...	...	...
Increase in public wage bill	...	...	...
Other	Temporary	0.4	−5.3
Revenue		22.5	3.3
PIT/exemptions/deductions	Permanent	4.9	5.4
Indirect tax reductions	Self-reversing	15.1	...
CIT/depreciation/incentives	...	...	...
Other	Permanent	2.5	−2.1
Memorandum items:			
Total cost		30.9	−0.3
In percent of GDP		1.5	0.0
United States[8]			
Expenditure		183.8	142.3
Infrastructure investment	Temporary	31.8	47.0
Support to SMEs and/or farmers	...	...	...
Safety nets	Temporary	77.0	13.8
Housing/construction support	...	...	...
Strategic industries support	...	...	...
Increase in public wage bill	...	...	...
Other	Temporary	75.0	81.5
Revenue		94.3	111.3
PIT/exemptions/deductions	Permanent	37.2	79.6
Indirect tax reductions	...	...	...
CIT/depreciation/incentives	Permanent	57.2	31.7
Other	...	...	...
Memorandum items:			
Total cost		283.2	257.3
In percent of GDP		2.0	1.8

[1]For some measure(s), the only information available is about their nature, but no estimate of their budgetary cost is available.

[2]Updated cost estimates are based on the breakdown of spending measures reported in February 2009.

[3]Cost is shown on a fiscal year basis. Includes only on-budget measures. Additional off-budget measures amount to 1.6 percent of GDP in 2009/10 (including 0.4 percent of GDP for bank recapitalization).

[4]The stimulus measures announced by the government will be partially offset by other "deficit-reducing" measures; IMF staff estimates assume that only part of revenue increasing measures from the November 2008 decree would be effective in 2009–11.

[5]Based on staff estimates of the cyclically adjusted general government balance. Additional stimulus in the form of infrastructure investment is being provided by the broader public sector, so that the total fiscal stimulus (as measured by the public sector borrowing requirement) is 4.2 percent of GDP in 2008, 6.2 percent in 2009, and 4.9 percent in 2010.

[6]Budget liquidity impact basis.

[7]Negative numbers refer to impact of offsetting measures.

[8]Excludes financial system rescue costs.

Appendix VII   Effect of Larger Debts on Interest Rates

Although empirical evidence on the impact of fiscal variables on interest rates is mixed, several studies find positive and significant effects (Table A7.1):

- The few studies focusing on "world" long-term real interest rates (average interest rates in the advanced economies) find that their main correlates are investment prospects (reflected in stock returns) and the monetary stance, with average fiscal deficits or debts playing an insignificant role in most estimates (Barro and Sala-i-Martin, 1990).

- Studies focusing on country-specific interest rates based on panels of countries or individual country time series find either insignificant or positive and significant effects. For member countries of the Organization for Economic Cooperation and Development (OECD), Ardagna, Caselli, and Lane (2007) find that a 1 percentage point increase in the ratio of the primary deficit to GDP is associated with a 10 basis point increase in nominal long-term (10-year) interest rates. The effect of an increase in public debt is estimated to be positive only for countries with large debts: a 10 percentage point increase in the debt/GDP ratio for a country with an initial ratio of 100 percent is associated with an increase of 20 basis points, whereas for a country with an initial ratio of 50 percent the effect is negligible. For the United States, studies that find a significantly positive effect put it in most cases in the range between 20–60 basis points for an increase in the budget deficit by 1 percentage point of GDP (Gale and Orszag, 2004).

- For emerging markets, variation in a country's sovereign bond spread is mainly correlated with changes in the average spread for all emerging markets; changes in country-specific fundamentals, including public debts or deficits, play a more limited role (see Mauro, Sussman, and Yafeh, 2006 for a review of this literature).

Methodological considerations suggest that the findings of these empirical studies should be viewed as a lower bound on the true effects. Observed fiscal deficits are an imperfect proxy for the concept of fiscal deficit that is expected to increase interest rates based on theory. Indeed, observed fiscal deficits are affected by a host of factors (to differing degrees in different countries) that cannot easily be controlled for in empirical studies (particularly for panels of countries), such as inflation, the position in the economic cycle, and varying quality of expenditures. With measurement error in the explanatory variable, the estimated coefficients are likely to reflect downward (i.e., "attenuation") bias. Moreover, the analysis is further complicated by the need to control for monetary policy, which may also respond to recessions at the same time as fiscal policy does.

Table A7.1 Studies on the Effects of Debt and Deficits on Interest Rates

Country	Predominantly Positive Significant Effect — Study	Numerical effect[1] Debt	Deficit	Mixed Effect — Study	Numerical effect[1] Debt	Deficit	Predominantly Insignificant Effect — Study	Numerical effect[1] Debt	Deficit
United States	Gale and Orszag (2004)[2]	0.04/0.06	0.25/0.35	Engen and Hubbard (2004)	0.03	0.03/0.19	Gale and Orszag (2004)	-0.03/0.04	0.02/0.17
	Dai and Phillipon (2004)		0.43/0.89 (VAR)	Engen and Hubbard (2004)	0.02 (VAR)	0.12 (VAR)	Plosser (1987)[5]	-0.07	
	Canzoneri, Cumby, and Diba (2002)		0.20/0.68	Perotti (2002)[8]		-1.41/-0.52 (VAR)	Evans (1987)		-0.08/0.13
	Miller and Russek (1996)		0.01/0.03	Perotti (2002)[9]		0.02/0.34 (VAR)	Evans (1985)[6]		-3.63/0.19
	Thomas and Abderrezak (1988)		0.64/1.55	Quigley and Porter-Hudak (1994)[11]	0.01		Mascaro and Meltzer (1983)	-0.07/0.02	
				Kim and Lombra (1989)[7]		-0.01/0.02	Hoelscher (1983)	0.09	
				Zahid (1988)[7]		-0.05/0.08	Plosser (1982)[10]	-0.01/-0.15	
				Tanzi (1985)	0.11/0.18	0.27 / 0.84			
Australia				Perotti (2002)[8]		0.09/0.45 (VAR)			
				Perotti (2002)[9]		-0.14/0.46 (VAR)			
Canada				Perotti (2002)[8]		-0.14/1.62 (VAR)	Evans (1987)		-0.04/0.02 (VAR)
				Perotti (2002)[9]		-0.41/0.25 (VAR)			
France							Evans (1987)		-0.03/0.07 (VAR)
Germany				Perotti (2002)[8]		0.46/1.86 (VAR)	Evans (1987)		-0.43/-0.17 (VAR)
				Perotti (2002)[9]		-0.21/0.75 (VAR)			
Italy				Cottarelli and Mecagni (1990)	0.13/2.01	0.2			
Japan									
United Kingdom				Perotti (2002)[8]		-0.57/0.95 (VAR)	Evans (1987)		-0.27/-0.23 (VAR)
				Perotti (2002)[9]		-0.07/0.34 (VAR)	Evans (1987)		-0.37/-0.36 (VAR)
Panel (advanced and emerging countries)	Aisen and Hauner (2008)		0.26/0.56				Cantor and Packer (1996)[3,4]	0.00/0.01	0.01/0.15
Panel (advanced countries)	Ardagna, Caselli, and Lane (2007)	0.002	0.1				Aisen and Hauner (2008)		-0.08
Panel (emerging countries)	Aisen and Hauner (2008)		0.24	Dell' Ariccia, Schnabel, and Zettelmeyer (2006)[12]	-0.02/-0.08	-0.92/1.27			
	Baldacci, Gupta, and Mati (2008)[3]		0.24/0.44	Mauro, Sussman, and Yafeh (2006)[3]		0.00/0.20			
	Eichengreen and Mody (1998)[3]	1.66							
	Min (1998)[3]	3.56							

Note: VAR is vector autoregression.
[1] Impact on interest rate (in percentage points) of a 1 percentage point of GDP increase unless otherwise indicated.
[2] Impact of projected fiscal variables on five-year-ahead interest rates.
[3] Dependent variable is spreads (percentage points) on U.S. dollar-denominated sovereign bonds over long-term interest rates on U.S. government bonds.
[4] Uses external debt (relative to exports).
[5] Uses shocks to the growth rate of real per capita public debt (1 percent).
[6] Uses the ratio of real deficit to real trend national income.
[7] Measure the impact of a $1 billion increase in the deficit.
[8] Effects of a 1 percent of GDP increase in public spending.
[9] Effects of a 1 percent of GDP increase in net taxes.
[10] Uses shocks to the growth rate of public debt (1 percent).
[11] Uses shocks to the announced increase in deficit (1 percent).
[12] Uses external debt (relative to GDP).

Appendix VIII   Japan: High Public Debt and Low Interest Rates

Japan's gross public debt has increased steadily since the early 1990s and now exceeds that of all other major advanced countries. Gross debt was close to 200 percent of GDP and net debt exceeded 90 percent of GDP at end-2007 (Figure A8.1). This reflects low economic growth and repeated efforts by the authorities to jumpstart the economy through fiscal stimuli.

At the same time, the government has continued to benefit from low financing costs. Long-term government bond yields gradually declined from 7 percent in 1990 to 1 percent in 2003 and have remained below 2 percent since. These yields have been consistently lower than for other G-7 countries.

Several factors, some of which may be seen as specific to Japan, could help reconcile low interest rates with large public debts.

- *High private saving rate.* The savings-to-GDP ratio of the private sector (including households, private corporations and private financial institutions), at 24 percent in 2007, is significantly above the average for member countries of the Organization for Economic Cooperation and Development (OECD) (17 percent).

- *Institutional restrictions.* Until the late 1990s, private pension funds were required to invest a significant share of their assets in domestic bonds; moreover, the special treatment of the postal system allows it to provide favorable yields that attract a significant share of retail deposits, which are partly channeled to the Japanese government bond market.

- *Home bias.* Despite the reduction/elimination of administrative and regulatory impediments to the acquisition or holding of foreign assets, home bias remains above the OECD average.

- *Net external position.* Japan is a large net creditor and does not depend on foreign creditors to finance its public debt.

Reflecting these factors, public debt is held almost exclusively by domestic investors (93 percent), notably domestic banks, life insurance companies, and several

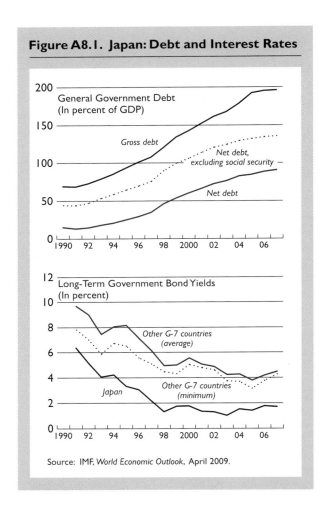

Figure A8.1. Japan: Debt and Interest Rates

General Government Debt
(In percent of GDP)

Gross debt

Net debt, excluding social security

Net debt

Long-Term Government Bond Yields
(In percent)

Other G-7 countries (average)

Japan

Other G-7 countries (minimum)

Source: IMF, *World Economic Outlook*, April 2009.

government-related entities (public financial institutions, pension funds, and the central bank).

Another hypothesis is that Japanese households may behave in a Ricardian manner: interest rates did not rise because households cut consumption to match the increasing dissaving of the government. This would also help explain why fiscal stimulus had limited impact in Japan.

Bibliography

Aisen, Ari, and David Hauner, 2008, "Budget Deficits and Interest Rates: A Fresh Perspective," IMF Working Paper 08/42 (Washington: International Monetary Fund).

Alesina, Alberto, 1988, "The End of Large Public Debts" in *High Public Debt: The Italian Experience*, ed. by Francesco Giavazzi and Luigi Spaventa (Cambridge, United Kingdom: Cambridge University Press).

Ardagna, Silvia, Francesco Caselli, and Timothy Lane, 2007, "Fiscal Discipline and the Cost of Public Debt Service: Some Estimates for OECD Countries," *The B.E. Journal of Macroeconomics*, Vol. 7, No. 1 (Topics), Article 28.

Baldacci, Emanuele, Sanjeev Gupta, and Amine Mati, 2008, "Is It (Still) Mostly Fiscal? Determinants of Sovereign Spreads in Emerging Markets," IMF Working Paper 08/259 (Washington: International Monetary Fund).

Barro, Robert, and Xavier Sala-i-Martin, 1990, "World Real Interest Rates," in *NBER Macroeconomics Annual*, ed. by Olivier Blanchard and Stanley Fischer (Cambridge, Massachusetts: MIT Press).

Black, Fischer, and Myron Scholes, 1973, "The Pricing of Options and Corporate Liabilities," *Journal of Political Economy*, Vol. 81, No. 3, pp. 637–54.

Burtless, Gary, 2009, "Stock Market Fluctuations and Retiree Incomes: An Update" (Washington: Brookings Institution).

Cantor, Richard, and Frank Packer, 1996, "Determinants and Impact of Sovereign Credit Ratings," *Economic Policy Review*, Vol. 2 (October), pp. 37–53.

Canzoneri, Matthew B., Robert E. Cumby, and Behzad T. Diba, 2002, "Should the European Central Bank and the Federal Reserve Be Concerned About Fiscal Policy?" paper presented at the Federal Reserve Bank of Kansas City's symposium on "Rethinking Stabilization Policy," Jackson Hole, Wyoming, August.

Carroll, Christopher D., Misuzu Otsuka, and Jirka Slacalek, 2006, "How Large Is the Housing Wealth Effect? A New Approach" NBER Working Paper No. 12746 (Cambridge, Massachusetts: National Bureau of Economic Research).

Cebotari, Aliona, 2008, "Contingent Liabilities: Issues and Practice," IMF Working Paper 08/245 (Washington: International Monetary Fund).

Congressional Budget Office (CBO), 2007, *The Long-Term Budget Outlook*, December (Washington).

———, 2008 *Monthly Budget Review*, December (Washington).

Cottarelli, Carlo, and Mauro Mecagni, 1990, "The Risk Premium on Italian Government Debt, 1976–88," IMF Working Paper 90/38 (Washington: International Monetary Fund).

Dai, Qiang, and Thomas Philippon, 2004, "Government Deficits and Interest Rates: A No-Arbitrage Structural VAR Approach" (New York: New York University).

Daniel, James, 1997, "Fiscal Aspects of Bank Restructuring," IMF Working Paper 97/52 (Washington: International Monetary Fund).

Daniel, James, Jeffrey M. Davis, and Andrew M. Wolfe, 1997, "Fiscal Accounting of Bank Restructuring," IMF Paper on Policy Analysis and Assessment 97/5 (Washington: International Monetary Fund).

Daniel, James, Jeffrey Davis, Manal Fouad, and Caroline Van Rijckeghem, 2006, *Fiscal Adjustment for Stability and Growth* (Washington: International Monetary Fund).

Dell'Ariccia, Giovanni, Isabel Schnabel, and Jeromin Zettelmeyer, 2006, "How Do Official Bailouts Affect the Risk of Investing in Emerging Markets?" *Journal of Money, Credit, and Banking*, Vol. 38, No. 7 (October), pp. 1689–1714.

Deposit Insurance Corporation of Japan. Available via the Internet: www.dic.go.jp/english/e_katsudou/e_katsudou1.html.

Eichengreen, Barry, and Ashoka Mody, 1998, "What Explains Changing Spreads on Emerging-Market Debt: Fundamentals or Market Sentiment?" NBER Working Paper No. 6408 (Cambridge, Massachusetts: National Bureau of Economic Research).

Engen, Eric, and R. Glenn Hubbard, 2004, "Federal Government Debts and Interest Rates," NBER Working Paper No. 10681 (Cambridge, Massachusetts: National Bureau of Economic Research).

European Commission (EC), 2006, *The Impact of Aging on Public Expenditure*, Special Report No. 1 (Brussels).

Evans, Paul, 1985, "Do Large Deficits Produce High Interest Rates?" *American Economic Review*, Vol. 75, No. 1 (March), pp. 68–87.

———, 1987, "Do Budget Deficits Raise Nominal Interest Rates? Evidence from Six Countries," *Journal of Monetary Economics*, Vol. 20, No. 2, pp. 281–300.

Fouad, Manal, Richard Hemming, Davide Lombardo, and Wojciech Maliszewski , 2004, "Fiscal Transparency and State-Owned Banks," in *The Future of State-Owned Financial Institutions*, ed. by Gerard Caprio and others (Washington: Brookings Institution).

Gale, William G., and Peter R. Orszag, 2004, "Budget Deficits, National Saving, and Interest Rates," *Brookings Papers on Economic Activity:2*, pp. 101–210.

Girouard, Nathalie, and Christophe André, 2005, "Measuring Cyclically-Adjusted Budget Balances for OECD Countries," OECD Economics Department Working Paper No. 434 (Paris: Organization for Economic Cooperation and Development).

Goodhart, Charles, 1999, "Monetary Policy and Debt Management in the United Kingdom: Some Historical Viewpoints," in *Government Debt Structure and Monetary Conditions*, ed. by K. Alec Chrystal (London: Bank of England).

Gray, Dale F., Robert C. Merton, and Zvi Bodie, 2007, "New Framework for Measuring and Managing Macrofinancial Risk and Financial Stability," NBER Working Paper No. 13607 (Cambridge, Massachusetts: National Bureau of Economic Research).

———, 2008, "New Framework for Measuring and Managing Macrofinancial Risk and Financial Stability," Harvard Business School Working Paper No. 09-015 (Revised) (Cambridge, Massachusetts: Harvard University, August).

Gray, Dale F., and Samuel Malone, 2008, *Macrofinancial Risk Analysis* (New York: John Wiley & Sons).

Gupta, Sanjeev, Benedict Clements, and Gabriela Inchauste, 2004, *Helping Countries Develop: The Role of Fiscal Policy* (Washington: International Monetary Fund).

Hauner, David, 2008, "The Macroeconomic Effects of Pension Reform," *Russian Federation: Selected Issues*, IMF Country Report No. 08/308 (Washington: International Monetary Fund).

Henriksson, Jens, 2007, "Ten Lessons About Budget Consolidation," Bruegel Essay and Lecture Series (Brussels: Bruegel).

Hoelscher, David, and Marc Quintyn, 2003, *Managing Systemic Banking Crises*, IMF Occasional Paper No. 244 (Washington: International Monetary Fund).

Hoelscher, Gregory P., 1983, "Federal Borrowing and Short Term Interest Rates," *Southern Economic Journal*, Vol. 50, No. 2 (October), pp. 319–33.

International Monetary Fund (IMF), 1986, *Manual on Government Finance Statistics* (Washington).

———, 2000, "Transition Economies: An IMF Perspective on Progress and Prospects." Available via the Internet: www.imf.org/external/np/exr/ib/2000/110300.htm.

———, 2001, *Manual on Government Finance Statistics* (Washington).

———, 2003, "Public Debt in Emerging Markets: Is It Too High?" Chapter 3, *World Economic Outlook, September 2003* (Washington).

———, 2005, "Is Public Debt in Emerging Markets Still Too High?" Box in *World Economic Outlook, September 2005* (Washington).

———, 2007a, *World Economic Outlook, October 2007* (Washington).

———, 2007b, *Manual on Fiscal Transparency* (Washington).

———, 2008a, *World Economic Outlook, October 2008: Financial Stress, Downturns, and Recoveries* (Washington).

———, 2008b, "The Fiscal Implications of Climate Change," Fiscal Affairs Department, February 22. Available via the Internet: www.imf.org/external/np/pp/eng/2008/022208.pdf.

———, 2009, "The Implications of the Global Financial Crisis for Low-Income Countries." Available via the Internet: www.imf.org/external/pubs/ft/books/2009/globalfin/globalfin.pdf.

Kim, Sun-Young, and Raymond E. Lombra, 1989, "Why the Empirical Relationship Between Deficits and Interest Rates Appears So Fragile," *Journal of Economics and Business*, Vol. 41, No. 3 (August), pp. 241–51.

Kroszner, Randall S., 2003, "Is it Better to Forgive Than to Receive? An Empirical Analysis of the Impact of Debt Repudiation" (Chicago: University of Chicago Graduate School of Business). Available via the Internet: http://gsbwww.uchicago.edu/fac/randall.kroszner/research/.

Kumar, Manmohan S., and Teresa Ter-Minassian, eds., 2007, *Promoting Fiscal Discipline* (Washington: International Monetary Fund).

Laeven, Luc, and Fabian Valencia, 2008, "Systemic Banking Crises: A New Database," IMF Working Paper 08/224 (Washington: International Monetary Fund).

Mascaro, Angelo, and Allan H. Meltzer, 1983, "Long- and Short-Term Interest Rates in a Risky World," *Journal of Monetary Economics*, Vol. 12, No. 4 (November), pp. 485–518.

Mauro, Paolo, Nathan Sussman, and Yishay Yafeh, 2006, *Emerging Markets and Financial Globalization: Sovereign Bond Spreads in 1870–1913 and Today* (Oxford and New York: Oxford University Press).

Mercer, 2009, "Pension Plan Deficit Hits Record $409 Billion for S&P 1500 Companies; Pension Expense May Rise," January 7, 2009. Available via the Internet: www.mercer.com/summary.htm?siteLanguage=100&idContent=1332250.

Merton, Robert C., 1973, "The Theory of Rational Option Pricing," *Bell Journal of Economics and Management Science*, Vol. 4, No. 1 (Spring), pp. 141–83.

Miller, Stephen M., and Frank S. Russek, 1996, "Do Federal Deficits Affect Interest Rates? Evidence from Three Econometric Methods," *Journal of Macroeconomics*, Vol. 18, No. 3 (Summer), pp. 403–28.

Min, Hong G., 1998, "Determinants of Emerging Market Bond Spread: Do Economic Fundamentals Matter?" Policy Research Working Paper No. 1899 (Washington: World Bank).

Morris, Richard, and Ludger Schuknecht, 2007, "Structural Balances and Revenue Windfalls: The Role of Asset Prices Revisited," ECB Working Paper No. 737 (Frankfurt: European Central Bank).

Munnell, Alicia, Jean-Pierre Aubry, and Dan Muldoon, 2008, "The Financial Crisis and State/Local Defined Benefit Plans," Issue Brief 8-19 (Chestnut Hill, Massachusetts: Center for Retirement Research at Boston College).

Organization for Economic Cooperation and Development (OECD), 2001, *Fiscal Implications of Aging*, Economics Department Working Paper No. 305 (Paris).

———, 2006, *Projecting OECD Health and Long-Term Care Expenditures: What Are the Main Drivers?* Economics Department Working Paper No. 5 (Paris).

———, 2008, "Pension Markets in Focus," Issue 5 (Paris).

Pension Benefit Guaranty Corporation (PBGC), 2008, *Annual Management Report: Fiscal Year 2008* (Washington).

Pension Protection Fund (PPF), 2008, *Annual Report and Accounts, 2007/2008*, London.

Perotti, Roberto, 2002, "Estimating the Effects of Fiscal Policy in OECD Countries," ECB Working Paper No. 168 (Frankfurt: European Central Bank).

Plosser, Charles I., 1982, "Government Financing Decisions and Asset Returns," *Journal of Monetary Economics*, Vol. 9, No. 3 (May), pp. 325–52.

———, 1987, "Fiscal Policy and the Term Structure," *Journal of Monetary Economics*, Vol. 20, No. 2 (September), pp. 343–67.

Quigley, Michael Regan, and Susan Porter-Hudak, 1994, "A New Approach in Analyzing the Effect of Deficit Announcements on Interest Rates," *Journal of Money, Credit and Banking*, Vol. 26, No. 4 (November), pp. 894–902.

Reinhart, Carmen, Kenneth Rogoff, and Miguel Savastano, 2003, "Debt Intolerance," *Brookings Papers on Economic Activity: 1*, pp. 1–62.

Spilimbergo, Antonio, Steve Symansky, Olivier Blanchard, and Carlo Cottarelli, 2008, "Fiscal Policy for the Crisis," IMF Staff Position Note 08/01 (Washington: International Monetary Fund).

Tanzi, Vito, 1985, "Fiscal Deficits and Interest Rates in the United States: An Empirical Analysis, 1960–1984," *Staff Papers*, International Monetary Fund, Vol. 32, No. 4 (December), pp. 551–76.

The Economist, "The Doctor's Bill," September 25, 2008.

Thomas, Lloyd B., Jr., and Ali Abderrezak, 1988, "Long-Term Interest Rates: The Role of Expected Budget Deficits," *Public Finance Quarterly*, Vol. 16, No. 3 (July), pp. 341–56.

United Kingdom Treasury, 2008, *Pre-Budget Report 2008*. Available via the Internet: http://prebudget.treasury.gov.uk/prebudget2008/.

United Nations, 2006, *World Population Prospects: The 2006 Revision*, United Nations Population Division (New York).

Verhoeven, Marijn, Victoria Gunnarsson, and Stéphane Carcillo, 2007, "Education and Health in G7 Countries: Achieving Better Outcomes with Less Spending," IMF Working Paper 07/263 (Washington: International Monetary Fund).

Whitehouse, 2007, *Pensions Panorama* (Washington).

World Bank, 2005, "Public Debt and Its Determinants in Market Access Countries" (unpublished; Washington).

———, 2006, *From Red to Grey: Report on Aging in Eastern Europe* (Washington).

Zahid, Khan Hasan, 1988, "Government Budget Deficits and Interest Rates: The Evidence Since 1971, Using Alternative Deficit Measures," *Southern Economic Journal*, Vol. 54, No. 3 (January), pp. 725–31.

Recent Occasional Papers of the International Monetary Fund

269. Fiscal Implications of the Global Economic and Financial Crisis, by a staff team from the Fiscal Affairs Department. 2009.

268. Structural Reforms and Economic Performance in Advanced and Developing Countries, by Jonathan D. Ostry, Alessandro Prati, and Antonio Spilimbergo. 2009.

267. The Role of the Exchange Rate in Inflation-Targeting Emerging Economies, by Mark Stone, Scott Roger, Seiichi Shimizu, Anna Nordstrom, Turgut Kişinbay, and Jorge Restrepo. 2009.

266. The Debt Sustainability Framework for Low-Income Countries, by Bergljot Bjørnson Barkbu, Christian Beddies, and Marie-Hélène Le Manchec. 2008.

265. Developing Essential Financial Markets in Smaller Economies: Stylized Facts and Policy Options, by Hervé Ferhani, Mark Stone, Anna Nordstrom, and Seiichi Shimizu. 2008.

264. Reaping the Benefits of Financial Globalization, by Giovanni Dell'Ariccia, Julian di Giovanni, André Faria, Ayhan Kose, Paolo Mauro, Jonathan D. Ostry, Martin Schindler, and Marco Terrones. 2008.

263. Macroeconomic Implications of Financial Dollarization The Case of Uruguay, edited by Marco Piñón, Gaston Gelos, and Alejandro López-Mejía. 2008.

262. IMF Support and Crisis Prevention, by Atish Ghosh, Bikas Joshi, Jun Il Kim, Uma Ramakrishnan, Alun Thomas, and Juan Zalduendo. 2008.

261. Exchange Rate Assessments: CGER Methodologies, by Jaewoo Lee, Gian Maria Milesi-Ferretti, Jonathan D. Ostry, Luca Antonio Ricci, and Alessandro Prati. 2008.

260. Managing the Oil Revenue Boom: The Role of Fiscal Institutions, by Rolando Ossowski, Mauricio Villafuerte, Paulo A. Medas, and Theo Thomas. 2008.

259. Macroeconomic Consequences of Remittances, by Ralph Chami, Adolfo Barajas, Thomas Cosimano, Connel Fullenkamp, Michael Gapen, and Peter Montiel. 2008.

258. Northern Star: Canada's Path to Economic Prosperity, edited by Tamim Bayoumi, Vladimir Klyuev, and Martin Mühleisen. 2007.

257. Economic Growth and Integration in Central America, edited by Dominique Desruelle and Alfred Schipke. 2007.

256. Moving to Greater Exchange Rate Flexibility: Operational Aspects Based on Lessons from Detailed Country Experiences, by Inci Ötker-Robe and David Vávra, and a team of IMF economists. 2007.

255. Sovereign Debt Restructuring and Debt Sustainability: An Analysis of Recent Cross-Country Experience, by Harald Finger and Mauro Mecagni. 2007.

254. Country Insurance: The Role of Domestic Policies, by Törbjörn Becker, Olivier Jeanne, Paolo Mauro, Jonathan D. Ostry, and Romain Rancière. 2007.

253. The Macroeconomics of Scaling Up Aid: Lessons from Recent Experience, by Andrew Berg, Shekhar Aiyar, Mumtaz Hussain, Shaun Roache, Tokhir Mirzoev, and Amber Mahone. 2007.

252. Growth in the Central and Eastern European Countries of the European Union, by Susan Schadler, Ashoka Mody, Abdul Abiad, and Daniel Leigh. 2006.

251. The Design and Implementation of Deposit Insurance Systems, by David S. Hoelscher, Michael Taylor, and Ulrich H. Klueh. 2006.

250. Designing Monetary and Fiscal Policy in Low-Income Countries, by Abebe Aemro Selassie, Benedict Clements, Shamsuddin Tareq, Jan Kees Martijn, and Gabriel Di Bella. 2006.

249. Official Foreign Exchange Intervention, by Shogo Ishi, Jorge Iván Canales-Kriljenko, Roberto Guimarães, and Cem Karacadag. 2006.

248. Labor Market Performance in Transition: The Experience of Central and Eastern European Countries, by Jerald Schiff, Philippe Egoumé-Bossogo, Miho Ihara, Tetsuya Konuki, and Kornélia Krajnyák. 2006.

247. Rebuilding Fiscal Institutions in Post-Conflict Countries, by Sanjeev Gupta, Shamsuddin Tareq, Benedict Clements, Alex Segura-Ubiergo, Rina Bhattacharya, and Todd Mattina. 2005.

246. Experience with Large Fiscal Adjustments, by George C. Tsibouris, Mark A. Horton, Mark J. Flanagan, and Wojciech S. Maliszewski. 2005.

245. Budget System Reform in Emerging Economies: The Challenges and the Reform Agenda, by Jack Diamond. 2005.

244. Monetary Policy Implementation at Different Stages of Market Development, by a staff team led by Bernard J. Laurens. 2005.

243. Central America: Global Integration and Regional Cooperation, edited by Markus Rodlauer and Alfred Schipke. 2005.

242. Turkey at the Crossroads: From Crisis Resolution to EU Accession, by a staff team led by Reza Moghadam. 2005.

241. The Design of IMF-Supported Programs, by Atish Ghosh, Charis Christofides, Jun Kim, Laura Papi, Uma Ramakrishnan, Alun Thomas, and Juan Zalduendo. 2005.

240. Debt-Related Vulnerabilities and Financial Crises: An Application of the Balance Sheet Approach to Emerging Market Countries, by Christoph Rosenberg, Ioannis Halikias, Brett House, Christian Keller, Jens Nystedt, Alexander Pitt, and Brad Setser. 2005.

239. GEM: A New International Macroeconomic Model, by Tamim Bayoumi, with assistance from Douglas Laxton, Hamid Faruqee, Benjamin Hunt, Philippe Karam, Jaewoo Lee, Alessandro Rebucci, and Ivan Tchakarov. 2004.

238. Stabilization and Reforms in Latin America: A Macroeconomic Perspective on the Experience Since the Early 1990s, by Anoop Singh, Agnès Belaisch, Charles Collyns, Paula De Masi, Reva Krieger, Guy Meredith, and Robert Rennhack. 2005.

237. Sovereign Debt Structure for Crisis Prevention, by Eduardo Borensztein, Marcos Chamon, Olivier Jeanne, Paolo Mauro, and Jeromin Zettelmeyer. 2004.

236. Lessons from the Crisis in Argentina, by Christina Daseking, Atish R. Ghosh, Alun Thomas, and Timothy Lane. 2004.

235. A New Look at Exchange Rate Volatility and Trade Flows, by Peter B. Clark, Natalia Tamirisa, and Shang-Jin Wei, with Azim Sadikov and Li Zeng. 2004.

234. Adopting the Euro in Central Europe: Challenges of the Next Step in European Integration, by Susan M. Schadler, Paulo F. Drummond, Louis Kuijs, Zuzana Murgasova, and Rachel N. van Elkan. 2004.

233. Germany's Three-Pillar Banking System: Cross-Country Perspectives in Europe, by Allan Brunner, Jörg Decressin, Daniel Hardy, and Beata Kudela. 2004.

232. China's Growth and Integration into the World Economy: Prospects and Challenges, edited by Eswar Prasad. 2004.

231. Chile: Policies and Institutions Underpinning Stability and Growth, by Eliot Kalter, Steven Phillips, Marco A. Espinosa-Vega, Rodolfo Luzio, Mauricio Villafuerte, and Manmohan Singh. 2004.

230. Financial Stability in Dollarized Countries, by Anne-Marie Gulde, David Hoelscher, Alain Ize, David Marston, and Gianni De Nicolò. 2004.

229. Evolution and Performance of Exchange Rate Regimes, by Kenneth S. Rogoff, Aasim M. Husain, Ashoka Mody, Robin Brooks, and Nienke Oomes. 2004.

228. Capital Markets and Financial Intermediation in The Baltics, by Alfred Schipke, Christian Beddies, Susan M. George, and Niamh Sheridan. 2004.

227. U.S. Fiscal Policies and Priorities for Long-Run Sustainability, edited by Martin Mühleisen and Christopher Towe. 2004.

226. Hong Kong SAR: Meeting the Challenges of Integration with the Mainland, edited by Eswar Prasad, with contributions from Jorge Chan-Lau, Dora Iakova, William Lee, Hong Liang, Ida Liu, Papa N'Diaye, and Tao Wang. 2004.

225. Rules-Based Fiscal Policy in France, Germany, Italy, and Spain, by Teresa Dában, Enrica Detragiache, Gabriel di Bella, Gian Maria Milesi-Ferretti, and Steven Symansky. 2003.

224. Managing Systemic Banking Crises, by a staff team led by David S. Hoelscher and Marc Quintyn. 2003.

223. Monetary Union Among Member Countries of the Gulf Cooperation Council, by a staff team led by Ugo Fasano. 2003.

222. Informal Funds Transfer Systems: An Analysis of the Informal Hawala System, by Mohammed El Qorchi, Samuel Munzele Maimbo, and John F. Wilson. 2003.

Note: For information on the titles and availability of Occasional Papers not listed, please consult the IMF's *Publications Catalog* or contact IMF Publication Services.